LAST TRAIN TO DIXIE

LAST TRAIN TO DIXIE

JACK TROTTER

To Clyde Wilson, Thomas Fleming,
Donald Livingston, and the late Aaron Wolf
for their unstinting generosity and encouragement.

Last Train To Dixie

Copyright © 2021 Jack Trotter

ALL RIGHTS RESERVED. No part of this publication may be reproduced, distributed, or transmitted in any form or by any means, including photocopying, recording, or other electronic or mechanical methods, or by any information storage and retrieval system without the prior written permission of the publisher, except in the case of very brief quotations embodied in critical reviews and certain other noncommercial uses permitted by copyright law.

Produced in the Republic of South Carolina by

SHOTWELL PUBLISHING LLC
Post Office Box 2592
Columbia, So. Carolina 29202

www.ShotwellPublishing.com

ISBN   978-1-947660-50-2

FIRST EDITION

10 9 8 7 6 5 4 3 2 1

Contents

Preface ix

"In All the Ancient Circles": Tourism and the Decline of Charleston's Elite Families 1

Of Monkeys and Mermaids 15

The Strange Career of Segregation 21

Grace King and the Prayers of Women 35

The Faces of Men 49

Zora Neale Hurston's White Mare 55

The Crossroads Merchants 61

GOP Country 69

Books Are for Blockheads! or, the Buckhead Bomber 79

The Flamingo Kid 87

Dixie for Dummies 97

Eating Crow 103

On Secession Hill 109

The Last Train: An Epilogue 119

Acknowledgements 135

Graveyard, Ruined Circular Church in Charleston, 1865.jpg

Preface

The essays collected in this volume span a period of 15 years. What ties them together is that they are all, in some fashion, concerned with southern matters: culture, politics, history, literature, music, folkways and religiosity. If they are a defense of the South, they are at times critical, as well. But they are all expressions of love and loyalty, for I am a Southerner born, and unashamedly so. My childhood home was situated on the eastern flank of Missionary Ridge, site of a tragic Confederate defeat, and I have lived most of my life in Dixie, never far from the whispers of ancestral voices. I hope that my readers will find that I have channeled those voices with the respect that they deserve.

More than half of the essays in this volume originally appeared in *Chronicles: A Magazine of American Culture* or in the *Abbeville Review*. The remainder, with one exception, began as talks given at the Abbeville Institute's annual Summer School at Seabrook Island, SC. All of the previously published material has been revised and/or updated.

While I am a southern partisan, I have not written exclusively for southern ears. I hope that I am not presumptuous in assuming that almost any reader from any walk of life may find something here that will edify or amuse. However, I can't promise not to give offense. I can only say, to quote the late John Graham Altman, III (whose political career I have celebrated in these pages), "I'm sorry [if] I caused pain to those whom I really caused pain."

Caveat emptor!

St. Michael's Church, Charleston, 1865

"In All the Ancient Circles":
Tourism and the Decline of Charleston's Elite Families

Few American cities have been so meticulously studied, admired or—for that matter—vilified as has Charleston. There are substantial reasons for this. During the colonial era Charleston, or Charles Town as it was then, rapidly emerged as the urban center of a plantation culture that would, by the middle of the 18th century, spread across the southern states to become a powerful but anachronistic slave-based economy standing athwart the predominant free-labor mercantilism that then characterized the developed economies of the Western world. During the decades prior to the American Revolution Charleston was one of America's wealthiest cities and its busiest seaport, its harbor bristling with the masts of schooners bound for Europe, laden with rice and indigo.

During the antebellum period Charleston's economic power was eclipsed by that of the rising capitalist cities of the northern seaboard, but it remained significant as a cultural and political nexus for an emergent southern nationalism and was the epicenter of the secessionist movement. The combined effects of the War for Southern Independence and Reconstruction were ruinous for the city and its elite families, and though many managed to recover properties lost to confiscation, they remained, for the most part, an impoverished ruling class whose control over the city depended less upon economic clout than upon its instincts for political leadership. By the turn of the 20th century Charleston had become, in the words of Owen Wister in his novel *Lady Baltimore*, a "little city of oblivion"—a city scarcely touched by the industrial and economic progress of the late 19th century, and haunted by the ghosts of a glorious and tragic past. While resistant to the commercial values of the rising New South, key figures among Charleston's elite families began, in the 1920s, to reinvent Charleston as a unique tourist destination. This gambit, which proved astonishingly successful, also proved, ironically, to be a major factor in the now almost certain disappearance of the city's ancient elite.

In 1860, on the eve of the War, Charleston remained—despite some decline in her economic status during the antebellum period—one of the wealthiest cities in the nation. According to the 1860 federal census 48 heads of household (1% of the free population) in Charleston reported wealth of $111,000 or more (ranging as high as $500,000), nine times the national average, while 168 (3% of the free population) reported wealth amounting to $51,000 or more—at least seven times higher than the national mean. Some 216 families, then, possessed over half of the total wealth in Charleston.[1] These families comprised the core of the Charleston elite, families whose surnames identified most of them as descendants of the first two or three generations of Carolina settlers. The majority of the elite heads of household were planters, many were merchants (especially cotton and rice factors) and others occupied traditional professions such as law and medicine. Virtually all of them were slaveholders.

When the Ordinance of Secession was passed on December 12, 1860 the Charleston elite had ruled the city for almost 200 years. A stroll through any of the well-preserved graveyards in Charleston or in the outlying plantation districts reveals just how frequently the offspring of the old families intermarried, reinforcing their hold upon wealth and power. Financially, politically, and socially they were an American "aristocracy" of astonishing cohesiveness, quite self-consciously cultivating the traditions of the English landed gentry; indeed, some of them were descended from younger sons of the gentry (both English and French). They sent their children to the same boarding schools, such as Madame Talvande's School for Young Ladies in Charleston, or Moses Waddel's Willington Academy for boys in the Abbeville District; they socialized in highly

---

[1] Michael P. Johnson, "Wealth and Class in Charleston," in *From the Old South to the New: Essays on the Transitional South*, eds. William J. Fraser and Winfred Moore. New York: Praeger, 1981. 66-67.

"IN ALL THE ANCIENT CIRCLES":
TOURISM AND THE DECLINE OF CHARLESTON'S ELITE FAMILIES

exclusive clubs such as the St. Cecilia Society, the Huguenot Society, and the St. Andrew's Society; and they dominated with an iron will the politics of the city and the state well into the antebellum years. Culturally, they were sometimes described by their contemporaries (and, later, by some historians) as self-indulgent, superficial and effete. While there is some truth in such observations, I would note that they were probably the most socially refined and hospitable elite society in America, and one that produced an impressive number of distinguished statesmen, military leaders, writers, naturalists, artists and scholars.

The combined effects of the War, Reconstruction and years of economic stagnation were devastating for Charleston and her first families. The Union blockade and constant shelling by enemy gunships had reduced the city to a shambles. Due to the blockade, exports of cotton and rice had been almost completely curtailed, basic necessities were scarce, and refugee planters returned to their plantations to find them often ransacked and burned, or simply confiscated and occupied by federally appointed overseers. Even family burial vaults were, in some cases, desecrated by marauding Union troops. The Alston and Pringle families, closely tied by marital alliances, may serve to illustrate the nature of the losses experienced by most of the Lowcountry elite. Prior to the War their properties included five plantations situated along the Waccamaw River and another, Runnymede, on the Ashley River, as well as one of the finest houses in the city, a King Street residence known today as the Miles Brewton House. Shortly after the War's end, they had been forced to sell off one of their estates to survive, three others had been confiscated by the Freedman's Bureau, Runnymede had been burnt to the ground, and a magnificent townhouse was occupied by Union officers. William Bull Pringle and his wife, Mary, were eventually able to reclaim the townhouse and one plantation, but, like most ex-Confederate landowners, William was forced to take the Oath of Allegiance and to pay confiscatory taxes before his property was restored.

While many of the Charleston elite were, like the Pringles, able eventually to recover some portion of their properties, their attempts to make the old plantations profitable once again were hampered by numerous difficulties—not the least of which was finding and paying for help under the free labor system. Many ex-slaves were reluctant to return to work, especially in the harsh conditions of the rice fields, and most of the Charleston landowners had invested heavily in Confederate currency, and thus were left effectively bankrupt by War's end. Even those plantations which managed to show a profit faced drastic reductions in production levels. Aside from the these factors, repeated flooding of the fields by hurricane-driven tides between 1885 and 1911 and competition from rice growers in Louisiana and Texas ensured that, by the second decade of the 20th century, the cultivation of rice, which had been the key component in the rise of the Lowcountry planters to social and political dominance of the region, was no longer a viable concern.

Nevertheless, the old families, for several reasons, managed to retain their social position and much of their traditional control of the city. They were well-educated, resourceful and long-accustomed to the maintenance of power. After the departure of occupation forces and the failure of Reconstruction, there was, moreover, no significant force in position to challenge their longstanding claim to rule. Charleston had never had a substantial middle class, and virtually all of the prominent merchants and lawyers were themselves tied by birth or marriage to the old families. Moreover, the resistance of the old guard to the unbridled capitalist ethos that reigned triumphant across America in the latter decades of the 19th century ensured that few new manufacturing interests gained a foothold in the old city. Historian John P. Radford has argued with reference to antebellum Charleston that "Forces regarded as potentially disruptive of the status quo were tenaciously opposed, including the powerful modernizing force of industrialization...." This same tenacious opposition persisted in the post-war era, and the "refusal to make concessions toward the American norm ..." ensured that post-bellum Charleston remained a city less interested in reconstruction (whether social or economic) than in *restoration* of the old order. While the New South movement was acclaimed in cities like Atlanta and Nashville, its unfettered embrace of industrialization on the northern model was regarded with a good

"IN ALL THE ANCIENT CIRCLES":
TOURISM AND THE DECLINE OF CHARLESTON'S ELITE FAMILIES

deal of suspicion by Charlestonians. While Charleston emerged from the ruins of the War as what Radford termed a "morphological anachronism," its steadfast refusal of modernization became the foundation for the heritage industry that would transform Charleston almost a century later. [2]

To be sure, there were prominent figures in the Charleston community who campaigned for modernization, and some who saw as early as the 1880s that Charleston was ideally situated to take financial advantage of the growing numbers of northern tourists who, during the Gilded Age, began streaming south in search of winter retreats and nostalgic locales. Several of the more progressive business leaders in the city, including George W. Williams and Frederick W. Wagener, began a campaign in 1888 to raise capital for a state-of-the-art hotel that would cater to the tourist trade. Such accommodations were sorely needed, since at that time the city could boast only one hotel of any size, the Charleston Hotel, which had been built in the antebellum era and had not been refurbished for decades. The campaign initially generated some enthusiasm, especially among younger businessmen, but fundraising efforts brought in only a quarter of the $1 million targeted sum. Promoters of the new hotel had also hoped to build the facility in the vicinity of the Battery (with its waterfront park, known traditionally as White Point Gardens), but local residents—almost exclusively old families—resisted any commercialization of the area.

At the turn of the new century, another scheme for promoting trade, attracting investment and bringing in tourists was floated and, eventually, realized. The South Carolina Interstate and West-Indian Exposition was backed, once again, by Frederick Wagener, a German-born businessman, and a cohort of men associated with the Young Men's Business League. Few of the old elite supported the scheme, but Wagener's deep pockets and credit with local banks, as well as a $50,000 allocation by the South Carolina General Assembly, resulted in the opening of the Exposition in 1901 on a site in the north end of the city along the Ashley River, an area

---

[2] See John P. Radford, "Social Structure and Urban Form: Charleston, 1860-1880," in *From the Old South to the New: Essays on the Transitional South*, eds. William J. Fraser and Winfred Moore. New York: Praeger, 1981 87-88.

which for many years had been the location of one of the premier horse racing tracks in the nation, the Washington Race Course, and which today is the site of Hampton Park and The Citadel military college. Although the Exposition managed to attract some 500,000 visitors over the course of several months, it was, in the words of historian Walter J. Fraser, Jr., a "picturesque disaster."

In retrospect it appears that the emergence of tourism as a major industry in Charleston was in large part the result of a compromise between the forces of modernization and preservation. One of the many ironies of this story is that the key figure in the preservation movement of the 1920s, Susan Pringle Frost, was herself a "progressive" who ran a real estate business. The granddaughter of Mary Alston Pringle, Frost grew up in the Miles Brewton House (then known as the Pringle House) and, as a young woman, served as executive secretary to Bradford Gilbert, chief architect of the West Indian Exposition. Her first practical ventures in preservation coincided with her ambitions as a realtor when she acquired and began refurbishing several properties on Tradd Street in the heart of the Charleston historic district. Frost was by no means a wealthy woman, and her efforts to restore such properties were often hampered by lack of funds, though she benefitted by a number of personal loans—most significantly by Irénée Dupont,[3] who for many years employed Frost's sister Rebecca as a family governess on the Duponts' Delaware estate. The Duponts were also instrumental in enabling the Frost sisters to establish sole ownership of the Miles Brewton House, a splendid example of the Charleston "double-house" in the Palladian style. There is no doubt that without Frost's efforts, the pioneering Society for the Preservation of Ancient Dwellings (today known simply as the Charleston Preservation Society), would never have been established. Founded in 1920, initially to raise funds for the restoration of the Joseph Manigault House on Meeting Street, the Society included many prominent members of old Charleston families, including Alston Deas and

---

[3] A useful account of Pringle's role in the preservation movement is Sidney R. Bland, *Preserving Charleston's Past, Shaping its Future: The Life and Times of Susan Pringle Frost*. Wesport, CT: Greenwood Press, 1994.

"IN ALL THE ANCIENT CIRCLES":
TOURISM AND THE DECLINE OF CHARLESTON'S ELITE FAMILIES

Thomas Stoney, who would become mayor of the city in 1923, serving two terms, actively promoting Charleston as "America's Most Historic City."

Outside the small circle of preservationists, Charlestonians were generally slow to recognize the long-term potential of preservation efforts. Many shared the view of former mayor and pro-development advocate John Patrick Grace, who ungenerously labeled the preservation movement as a "mania for mummies." Grace regarded the preservationists as driven primarily by personal nostalgia for a past long since dead. "Why not," he asked, "awaken with this mercenary reverence for old things also the enterprise which made these old things?"[4] In fact, Frost and her cadre of preservation activists were not opposed to development, but sought to restrict its encroachment upon the most historic precincts of the city, where demolition of old "dwellings" and many other buildings was, by the 1920s, advancing at an alarming rate. While the preservationists' reverence for the past was, indeed, fraught with personal and familial associations, they also recognized that Charleston's architectural riches were a patrimony of enduring value, not simply for a privileged elite, but for the city and the nation. Frost insisted on more than one occasion that to eradicate the physical remains of the past was to eradicate the possibility of historical memory itself.

Throughout the 1920s and into the Great Depression era, tourist numbers in Charleston gradually rose. Initially, this had little to do with preservation. Tourists from the North came primarily for the warm winters and the spring Azalea Festival, and many of them were rather well-heeled visitors who not infrequently became purchasers of Frost's restored or refurbished old dwellings in the southeastern quadrant of the city. In fact, wealthy Northerners had been buying up Lowcountry properties for some years, including numerous old plantations which had been occupied by Charleston families since the colonial period. These now began to pass into the hands of millionaires like the Guggenheims, the Roosevelts, the Luces, the Duponts and many others who were captivated by

---

4 Stephanie Yuhl. *A Golden Haze of Memory: The Making of Historic Charleston.* Chapel Hill: The University of North Carolina, 2005. 42.

their romantic settings and sought them out as seasonal retreats. In most cases such properties were sold out of dire financial need, and one can discern a hint of resentment in a remark made by William Watts Ball, scion of one of the city's oldest families and editor of the city's leading newspaper, the *News and Courier*, in 1929, "Indeed, the odor of genteel Yankee wealth, while not suffocating, is pervading Charleston."[5] But as City Hall stepped up its campaign to publicize Charleston, and as more and more northern and midwestern newspapers reported on the charms of the city, the tourists became increasingly middle-class and arrived in greater numbers. In 1931 the city enacted a zoning ordinance, the first of its kind in the nation, that established a clearly defined historic district and made provisions for legal action against developers or property owners who violated the provisions of the ordinance. By 1934 over a quarter of a million visitors annually made tourism the single largest source of income for the city. While World War II interrupted the tourist influx, the affluence of the post-war era ensured that tourism would remain a viable industry for the city, though throughout the 50s and 60s the number of visitors remained manageable and the character of the city was not notably altered by their seasonal presence.

While early preservation efforts were often piecemeal—directed at rehabilitating specific streets or restoring endangered houses—the emergence of the Historic Charleston Foundation in 1947 inaugurated a new, more comprehensive vision for the preservation of the city's history. Like the Preservation Society, it has for more than half a century worked to preserve historic homes, but it has also developed an extensive economic, environmental and educational agenda, and has been an important force in extending the scope of the city's zoning laws and in formulating its long-range tourism planning. The Foundation, too, was at its outset led and organized by the Charleston old guard, and flourished under the guidance of Frances Ravenel Edmunds, who remained its president until 1985. As a result of the work of the Preservation

---

[5] Michael P. Johnson, "Wealth and Class in Charleston," in *From the Old South to the New: Essays on the Transitional South*, eds. William J. Fraser and Winfred Moore. New York: Praeger, 1981. 66-67.

"IN ALL THE ANCIENT CIRCLES":
TOURISM AND THE DECLINE OF CHARLESTON'S ELITE FAMILIES

Society, the Foundation, the city's Board of Architectural Review and a number of other private and municipal entities, Charleston has today become one of the most admired and emulated examples of urban and historical reclamation in the world, written up in countless journal and magazine articles and currently attracting over four million visitors each year. Today, the city is so routinely placed by *Conde Nast* and other travel magazines at the top of the list of America's most desirable tourist destinations, that the news is greeted by Charlestonians with a yawn and a shrug—and often enough with a sigh. For in recent years the character of the city has been transformed, and not always for the better.

This transformation was not by happenstance. The turning point was the election of Joseph P. Riley, Jr. in 1975, the mayor who directed the city's destiny for over forty years. That election was significant for a number of reasons. For over a century the city's political leadership, and especially the mayor's office, had been dominated—with rare exceptions—by the so-called "Broad Street Ring," a cabal of powerful lawyers and realtors, most of them connected to or allied with the old families. The Rileys, however, were not old money, though Joseph Riley, Sr., had established a successful insurance firm on Broad St. in 1936. In the mid-1970s the city faced formidable problems. Despite the ongoing progress of the preservation movement, much of the city was still dilapidated and unemployment levels were worrisome, especially among blacks. More pressing, the city's crime rates were dangerously high. Riley, only 32 at the time, ran a very astute campaign. The Rileys were a Catholic family and he drew heavily on the Catholic vote (just as the city's first Catholic mayor, John Grace, had in 1911), but he also formed a coalition of politically progressive old money, pro-development realtors, and African Americans. Certainly, there was stiff resistance to the Riley coalition among the more conservative traditional elite, but during his first term in office Riley moved quickly to make good on his promises: building new parks and recreation centers, especially in minority neighborhoods, appointing a highly effective black chief-of-police, Reuben Greenberg, and promoting a policy of "balanced" growth and urban reclamation. To achieve the latter goal he drew heavily on the Carter administration's Urban Development Action Grant (UDAG) program, designed for the reclamation of deteriorating districts of American cities. Also, among the achievements of his first term in office were the Spoleto Festival U.S.A., now an internationally celebrated arts festival, and the Charleston Place project. The first of these, Spoleto, has by virtually universal acclaim been an astounding success for the city. Aside from a few years in the late 1970s and early 80s the festival has been profitable and consistently draws internationally celebrated performers while maintaining an enviable balance between traditional and *avant-garde* styles in music, theater, dance and opera.

The Spoleto Festival, along with the emergence of Charleston as a center of *nouvelle* southern cuisine, has done a great deal to enhance the city's reputation as a cultural mecca. The Charleston Place project, has, on the other hand, been more controversial. One of Mayor Riley's pet projects, Charleston Place was promoted in the late 1970s as a major hotel and shopping hub that would function as an anchor for the expansion of the tourism industry. Much of the original resistance to the idea, especially from preservationists, was due to the location chosen for the project, just across from the old City Market and situated between Meeting and King Streets, the two main arteries running the length of the Charleston peninsula. The plan required the demolition of a number of buildings considered of historic significance, though defenders of the plan argued that the block chosen for demolition had become an eyesore and that the buildings in question were rapidly becoming derelict. After several years of squabbling, and compromise, Charleston Place was completed in 1985. Certainly, as an economic venture, the project has vindicated the mayor's plan. Since its completion, King Street has become once again a thriving commercial artery. However, critics note that Charleston Place, which caters exclusively to the well-to-do, has been a major catalyst in stimulating the soaring property values in the area, where many family and locally-owned businesses have been replaced by *chic* chain stores and upscale shops selling luxury items that that the average Charlestonian

"IN ALL THE ANCIENT CIRCLES":
TOURISM AND THE DECLINE OF CHARLESTON'S ELITE FAMILIES

couldn't begin to afford. For better or worse, Charleston Place has become a symbolic reminder for many that tourism and real estate now drive the city's economy.

For over a century after 1865, the founding families and others who gained prominence during the colonial and early antebellum eras remained largely in control of Charleston's economy, politics and culture (though that culture was influenced by many factors, especially the presence of a large black population). Today, their control of the city is slipping away irrevocably, and in part because of the flourishing of the tourist industry. To be sure, some of the established families have benefitted by tourism, though not, in most cases, directly. As millions of tourists flow into the city each year, and as the city has become an increasingly attractive place to reside, a significant number of those visitors choose to invest in Charleston properties, or to establish businesses—just as in the past, but in greater numbers. While exact figures are hard to come by, it is well-known that hundreds of residential properties in the French Quarter and the South of Broad areas are now owned by people from "off"—that is, people who have no history in the city. Many of those same properties were sold off by old Charleston families, some of them for prices unheard of prior to the Riley regime.

One of the sources I spoke to in the course of researching this article, let us call him "Corvo"—a gentleman whose family has been prominent in Charleston since the 1820s—noted that many of the old families who sold off their plantations in the latter part of the 19th century became exclusively city dwellers, "often going into the professions." Some "invested their money well, others frittered it away and lost status." For a while their "old family" connections kept them afloat socially, "but if subsequent generations did not restore their wealth they slowly faded out of the ranks." As real estate prices began to rise in the 1970s and subsequent decades, many found the offers for their Charleston properties too lucrative to refuse. Corvo notes that "after hurricane Hugo in 1989 ... [many] of the real old Charlestonians were moving to nursing homes [or] leaving downtown. Some of their children took their places, but even they in many cases could not handle the financial demands of large old houses, private school tuition, and social pressures." So, of course, they unloaded their properties: "By the time the recession of the early 1990s was over the wealthy from 'off' began to take over while my contemporaries sold out and moved to the suburbs." Some of them did well enough to move to exclusive communities like Kiawah, one of the Sea Islands just south of the city, or to nearby Sullivan's Island. Others remained in the city and, through prudent investment—often in real estate—managed to maintain their status. But their numbers are dwindling, and, as Corvo notes, the "real money" today is from "off."

In America, as in much of the capitalist world today, power almost always follows, or is closely allied with, wealth. In Charleston over the last few decades, according to Corvo, the "big money" lies in the hands of the "newcomers, ... the people who have made it in corporate America, or [in] hedge funds and investments and who have given generously to the Gibbes Museum, Spoleto, etc." Indeed, a glance at the names on the boards of directors at many of Charleston's high-profile non-profit institutions, like the Gibbes or the Historic Charleston Foundation, reveals that the leadership is shifting to new money from elsewhere, to those who make the most generous contributions. In the business sector, similar changes have been occurring. Corvo recalls that up through most of the 1960s "there were three banks in Charleston," and all were controlled by Charlestonians. But in the 1970s "the banks began slowly replacing their Charleston leadership with outsiders that were more professional and could compete with [the leadership at] the new banks in the city."

Charleston's most visible institutions of higher education have undergone comparable changes, as well. The College of Charleston was, until recent decades, largely a city and regional institution, deeply imbued with the city's heritage and focused on providing a traditional classical education. Many of its instructors over the years, like Theodore Jervey, came from prominent local families. Today, the College has gone upscale, changed its name to the University of Charleston, recruits its student body and professoriate from a nation-wide pool of applicants, and offers a curriculum that differs very little from any college in America. Indeed, in virtually every sector of the city's public life

"IN ALL THE ANCIENT CIRCLES":
TOURISM AND THE DECLINE OF CHARLESTON'S ELITE FAMILIES

affluent newcomers are highly visible. According to the *Post and Courier*, Charleston is rapidly overtaking cities like Palm Beach in the growth of liquid assets, a development indicated by the proliferation of Fortune 500 investment firms in the city.

For the first time since the 1860 census was taken Charleston has become a wealthy city again, and while much of that wealth is in the possession of a new moneyed class, some of the old Charleston families have thrived: the Hamiltons, Colemans, Maybanks, Stoneys, Prioleaus, Rhetts and others, including the Manigault family, who still own the *Post and Courier* and a small constellation of media outlets across the country. Of the old families that have survived and who remain influential in the city, most, according to Corvo, are Republicans, but that in itself is little guarantee that they remain a genuinely conservative elite. Many still maintain memberships at St. Michael's or St. Philip's, episcopal churches founded in the 1680s, or at the nearby Huguenot Church. Some of the old traditions are maintained, especially on the distaff side, yet much of the graciousness and high aristocratic breeding of the past is fading. After the catastrophic losses of 1861-65 Charleston's impoverished elite still had some claim to the name of "aristocracy." Their fortunes were still rooted in the land, not in the mercenary wealth of the capitalist order. "Today," Corvo laments, "money is the real barometer by which one maintains [one's] status. My mother used to say that Charleston was the one place [where] money could not buy social status. That is no longer the case...." In an 1870 letter to Edward McCrady, Jr., the great Charleston novelist Gilmore Simms, then near the end of his life, cautioned against "unwise, precipitate concessions to the claims of the Union conquerors. He spoke of those "rights which are ... still inherent, still sacred, still capable to save us, if we do not fling them away in our eagerness to haste after flesh pots. Let us hold ourselves aloof; touch not, handle not, taste not anything in common with our invaders; keep up communion among ourselves, as well as we can, in all the ancient circles." [6] The "rights" to which Simms referred were property rights and the right of self-rule. Led by writers like

---

6 *The Letters of Gilmore Simms*, Vol. 6. Columbia, SC: The University of South Carolina Press, 2012. 272

McCrady, Theodore Jervey, and, later, William Watts Ball—all scions of the old families—Charleston, during the latter decades of the 19th century and well into the 20th, reasserted its rights while remaining suspicious of the capitalist "flesh pots." Imbued with the spirit of the Lost Cause, the old families turned inward and embraced their heritage unapologetically, and did, indeed, remain "aloof" from the American way of getting and spending. But even as they did so, they remained visible leaders of their city.

Today, the old families which remain, remain silent. They have no public voice. They raise no banner of resistance against the ever-expanding power of the federal monolith. The only member of the old guard who aspires to a position of public leadership today is Thomas Ravenel, Jr., a convicted drug dealer, womanizer, reality tv star, and a barely literate boor, whose wealth was, of course, made primarily in the real estate market. This is a rather sad endnote to a long and admirable history, but as Corvo says, "just like ordinary folks, old families rise, prosper and fall." In the wake of Mayor Riley's last term of office, a new elite has begun to consolidate its hold on Charleston, beginning with the June 2020 removal of the historic statue of John C. Calhoun, South Carolina's greatest public servant. Clearly, Charleston's brave new elite will not allow anything to discourage the tourist flood. For the tourism industry is for modern Charleston what the rice culture was for the old city, a cash cow that everyone milks while turning their noses the other way.

OF MONKEYS AND MERMAIDS

February 3, 1843

Charleston

My Dearest Sabrina,

 Having momentarily sated what you once aptly termed my "Herculean appetite for lethargy," I rouse myself dutifully to pen this somewhat belated missive, all too aware that you, my beloved sister, must be starved for news of Charleston. Everyone enquires about you, of course, & I invariably assure them that motherhood flatters you & that you and your amiable Yankee husband grow daily more prosperous. But, alas, I have little in the way of gossip to retail. I dine once a week, as always, at the Planter's Hotel with a few of my bachelor familiars, where we remind one another of the horrors attendant upon the matrimonial state. Aside from that comforting ritual, I socialize very little, pursue my bookish habits, & return most invitations with some politic expedient or other. My gout seems to be flaring up a good deal of late!

 Speaking of matrimonial matters, I do have one alarming scrap of gossip for you. You will no doubt be shocked to learn that your old schoolmate at Madame Talvande's, Sue Petigru, has recently announced her engagement to none other than Mr. Henry King. It is widely supposed that Susan will now retire her quiver of poisoned darts & terrorize our drawing rooms no more. If I were a betting man, I would wager that, contrary to popular opinion, we will hear more from our brilliant Susan after she has managed to depose her King. Indeed, it is rumored that she is at work on a novel, a series of satirical portraits that, if ever they see the light of day, will make our respectable matrons squirm.

Now, on to the entrée. You know how fond I am of those itinerant shows that feature freaks of nature or prodigies of one kind or another. Flea circuses, bearded ladies, talking automata, prestidigitators, ventriloquists—all of them provide me an exquisite delight that no doubt bespeaks some deformity of my own character. But *life*, my dear, is so *fatiguing* & these entertainments are so refreshingly absurd! Some swear by Brown's Iron Bitters, while I find perfect rejuvenation in observing the amazing Signor Blitz produce a lady's glove from a loaf of bread. Imagine my rapture, then, when I came across a notice in the *Mercury* on January 17, announcing a Grand Exhibition of the Wonders of Nature, featuring a "MERMAID recently taken near the Feejee Islands." You will recall, of course, my youthful infatuation with sea sirens. I required no further incentive to view this fabulous creature at the first opportunity, but my appetite was sharpened by the rather extravagant claims made by the promoter of this event. His Feejee Mermaid, it seems, having been previously exhibited in New York and Boston, "had utterly dispelled the doubts of thousands of naturalists and scientific persons regarding the real existence of such an animal." Was this not tantamount to throwing down the gauntlet? Could this enterprising Yankee be unaware that our somnolent Charleston is a veritable viper's nest of said naturalists?

With mounting anticipation, then, I made my way up King Street on the opening day of the exhibition, where I found, to my dismay, that a long queue had already formed before the Masonic Hall. I took my place along with the usual motley assemblage of truant schoolboys, vagrant apprentices, parlor maids, and mechanics (and not a few of our own class!). Mounted over the main entry of the Hall was a rather large signboard bearing the image of a mermaid, her naked torso rising sensuously above the water. As I beheld that smiling visage, I smiled inwardly to recall Heine's *Lore Ley*— "A Siren lost in her dreaming, combing her golden hair."

Distracted by such juvenile reveries, at length I found myself gazing upon a sort of glass dome, in which was encased the sea maiden. The contrast between the intoxicating image still lingering in my mind's eye & that which now assaulted my vision was unnerving! Here was hideous monstrosity! This was no mermaid, but a shriveled, brown sea hag, no more than three feet long, with a head of hair that resembled nothing so much as dried seaweed. And yet, one could not deny that this disgusting *thing* fulfilled, in the strictly anatomical sense, the requirements of a mermaid. From the waist down, it was all scaly fishtail; above, one might at least descry the lineaments of the female sex in its misshapen dugs. I assure you, Sabrina, that I, who *never* do hurry, flew from that hellish sight as quickly as my dignity would allow.

Of course, I was never so credulous as to believe that I would see an actual mermaid. I had hoped, though, for some credible piece of cozenage. In any event, I congratulated myself on my prescience when, on the following day, a communication appeared in the *Mercury* from someone styling himself "No Humbug." This writer, clearly incensed, pronounces the Mermaid a "contemptible hoax." The crux of his proof? The Mermaid is "rather a clumsy affair—the seams are not sufficiently covered to conceal the point of union between Fish and Monkey, even through a glass case. Our Yankee neighbors usually show more ingenuity, and they ought to have recollected that although we poor simpletons of Charleston are a long way off from the Banks of New Foundland, we are not to be imposed upon by the tail of a Codfish!" Our "No Humbug" then offers a bargain. If the "man who exhibits the Mermaid" will allow the "naturalists of Charleston" to take the "smoke-dried affair" out of her glass case and examine her, they will be delighted to issue a certificate of authenticity, should the Lady in question prove to be, indeed, the "greatest wonder in nature."

Now, I am quite sure, Sabrina, that this "No Humbug" is none other than our old acquaintance, Rev. Bachman, who was never so amusing, as I recall, at the supper table. Moreover, I have since had it on reliable authority that the Mermaid's agent is a rascal by the name of Alanson Taylor, said to be the uncle of that Master of Humbug, Phineas T. Barnum, whose museum of wonders I believe you visited on your last trip to New York. Mr. Taylor lost no time in leaping to the defense of his loathsome exhibit, & what a transparent piece of knavery was his first of several letters to the *Mercury*. Of course, he refused to remove the Mermaid from her glass dome on the grounds that she might be "defaced" (though God knows that could result only in dramatic improvement!), and repeatedly charges his accuser with a lack of "moral courage" for failing to reveal his true identity. He then offers to pay $500 if "No Humbug" will "present to our notice a Baboon or any other animal of the monkey species, which has a head and shoulders like this Mermaid's."

However ignorant Mr. Taylor may be of our little corner of the world, he is no doubt perfectly aware that Baboons, or anything resembling the "monkey species," are not known to frequent the Carolinas—unless, of course, one includes those apes of fashion who promenade along the Battery each evening. (I confess that I agree with the Comte de Buffon that the ape is a singular animal, one upon which we cannot gaze without, perforce, reflecting upon ourselves!) Thus, Mr. Taylor is not unlike a man who invites his friends to dine upon pickled tripe, knowing full well that they will hastily recall prior engagements.

Our Rev. Bachman, of course, was never a man to leave well enough alone. After the controversy spilled over into the pages of the *Courier*, which resoundingly endorsed that unprepossessing Lady's authenticity, he called up the heavy scientific artillery. When the *Courier* would not publish his scathing denunciations, he found the editors of the *Mercury* more than willing. To spare you the tedium of a full account, my impatient sister, I will merely relate the gist of the matter. Upholding the cause of science as well as "truth & morals," "No Humbug" asserts that the "pretended mermaid" is nothing that could possibly exist in nature. Her nostrils, clearly those of a mammal, declare that she breathes through lungs and is warm blooded; her nether parts, however, indicate that she is "an animal that breathed through gills and was cold blooded." According to our ecclesiastical naturalist, the "system of nature is beautiful, harmonious, and perfect in all its parts, and Naturalists feel it a duty to defend it against those who, with barbarous hands, would mutilate the symmetry of her works."

Indeed, what I beheld beneath that glass dome was certainly a vile caricature, but I am afraid, Sabrina, that I do not quite share Rev. Bachman's benign view of nature's perfection. Does not nature herself routinely beget grotesqueries every bit as ghastly as our Feejee Mermaid? Does not my beloved Pliny speak of a tribe of dog-headed, barking men, & of headless men with eyes in their shoulders? *Haec atque talia ex hominum genere ludibria sibi, nobis miracula ingeniosa fecit natura*! Nevertheless, I am inclined to agree that the Mermaid is doubtlessly a fraud.

Poor Mr. Taylor! After several days of rough treatment, he fled with his smoke-dried darling to Savannah, from whence he fired one last riposte at his accuser. "When, Sir," he blusters, "did God reveal to you what kind of animals he had power to create and what not? Into what kind he could infuse life and cause them to live and breathe in one element; and what kind he could not?" In short, the petty taxonomies of our naturalists are no match for the creative genius of the Divine Artificer. But no doubt suspecting that some *evidence* might be in order, Mr. Taylor proffers the example of the green turtle. "Has he not 'nostrils' (and no gills) through which he breathes like land animals? Yet has he not got 'fins' and not feet, by the aid of which he moves; and not withstanding his fins, is he not 'warm blooded'?"

Green turtles, indeed! What a desperate piece of humbuggery! And, yet, Sabrina, I confess that my deepest sympathies lie with Mr. Taylor. I fear that our scientific men are become altogether too evangelical. For all their pious talk of the beauties of the "system of nature," I suspect that they are intent upon stripping our common Mother of every last vestige of her charm! Rev. Bachman claims no other motive than to expose a fraud, but it is clear to me that there is no place in his "system" for mermaids, or gremlins, or faeries, or unicorns—not to speak of angels & devils! If superstition is to be eradicated, then how long can religion itself continue to flourish? Both, surely, rely upon our willingness to believe in a realm of mystery & miracle which our zealous empirics cannot abide. In its place they would erect a sterile idol called "Scientific Truth" and have us all grovel before it.

Bah! Speaking for myself, I prefer to believe in Oberon's mermaid, riding the waves upon her dolphin's back, "uttering such dulcet and harmonious breath / That the rude sea grew civil at her song."

But enough of that, dear sister. I must nap.

Ever your fond brother,

Thomas [1]

---

[1] While it should be obvious that the speaker in this letter is a purely fictitious creation, the historical context is quite real. P.T. Barnum's hideous mermaid did, indeed, visit in Charleston in 1843, and the controversy which erupted over her purported authenticity was equally real. The reader who wishes the explore this topic might begin with Jan Bondeson's book *The Feejee Mermaid and Other Essays in Natural and Unnatural History* (2014).

THE STRANGE CAREER OF SEGREGATION

In the beginning, there was no segregation, certainly not in the sense that we commonly use that term today. Consider in evidence our southern distinctiveness, which is rooted in a folk culture compounded of black and white influences: our modes of speech; our rich cuisines and rites of conviviality; our varied and original musicality; our arts and crafts; our story-telling traditions; our unbridled passion for sport; our legends and superstitions; our humor; and our attitudes towards work and leisure. From the South Carolina Sea Islands to the Piney Woods of east Texas, these overlapping folk traditions thrive, and, despite many local variations and anomalies, they bind Southerners together into a unique people, regardless of race or class. Nor is southern folk culture exclusively a product of the *rural* South. Charles Joyner, in his *Shared Traditions* (1999), insists that for the most part folk culture is portable, and also thrives (and is sometimes transformed) in urban milieus.

As more than one historian has noted, African slavery was a relatively late development in the northern states. When slaves arrived in places like New York or Pennsylvania, they entered long-established communities and had very little role in shaping the local cultures. Indeed, in the North, they were never more than 10% of the slave population of colonial North America. In the South, slaves were among the earliest settlers. Blacks and whites in the South have always been fellow travelers, and have as often as not lived cheek by jowl, at least until recently.

Nowhere is the reality of African influence so forcefully illustrated as in the history of Charleston, where enslaved Africans arrived with their Barbadian masters in the 1670s. *Together* they cleared the swamps, *together* they shared the perils of the Yemassee War and harvested the first crop of Carolina Gold, creating the rice culture which would make Charleston one of the busiest and wealthiest ports in the New World. The folk culture that emerged in the Carolina Lowcountry was a unique blend of European and African practices. If the foodstuffs which graced the table of the "big house" were more plentiful than the fare consumed in the slave quarters, the recipes were often much the same, and often African in origin (think yams and hominy grits). If black slaves brought with them indigenous musical styles, they also adopted European instruments like the fiddle (without which no Christmas feast on Lowcountry plantations would have been complete). Similarly, the Lowcountry dialect of the masters was a fusion of English, West African and Caribbean speech, as was the "Gullah" spoken by the slave population, though it was more distinctively African in its forms and rhythms.

Most importantly, perhaps, blacks and whites in Carolina shared a common piety, and if the black expression of that shared faith veered toward a more potent "enthusiasm," it is also true that the plaintive hymns of the enslaved subtly shaped and informed the spiritual lives of the masters. It might be interesting to attempt a counterfactual history in which a strict segregation had been imposed upon the African population from the start—something not unlike the Jim Crow regime which came later—and to consider whether this shared and distinctive southern culture could ever have flourished. But "what if" histories are a fool's game (or, as the Gullah proverb would have it: "Dog got four feets but can only walk one road.").

While colonial and antebellum southern society was a hierarchically arranged system of white dominance, one which involved some degree of *exclusion*, segregation was not a significant factor. What was true of the Carolina Lowcountry was true across the South. To understand the extent of the integrated lives of blacks and whites in the Old South, it will be helpful to consider how their lives played out daily on those plantation—large, middling, and small—that were the site of the predominant mode of life, keeping in mind that roughly only 10% of the Southern population, until well into the 20th century, resided in towns or cities. The key idea here is the idea of the plantation *household*, which was so much more than a private dwelling. As Elizabeth Fox-Genovese has written in her book *Within the Plantation Household* (1988), "[It] contained within [itself] the decisive relations of production and reproduction." And each of these was part of a vast network of such households that pervasively shaped the character of southern society. In the North a separation of spheres had already emerged, in keeping with the evolution of the capitalist market economy, which divided the private realm—the realm of familial affections— from the public sphere of production. Any attempt to understand southern society without drawing this contrast is doomed to fall well short of the mark. In the southern household, masters, mistresses, their children, and their slaves all considered themselves a part of an extended *family*, sharing both familial affection and the labor which was essential to their flourishing.

Naturally, most 21st century Americans would scoff at such an assertion. How could those who were subjected to such a brutal and unjust system genuinely consider themselves part of the plantation family? But the evidence for this goes well beyond proslavery polemics or the idealized worlds of Lost Cause fiction; it is borne out not only in the diaries and letters of masters and mistresses, but in voluminous slave narratives taken down after the War. This is not to say that slaves did not often resent and resist the power of the master, or that they preferred their enslavement to freedom; rather, it seems that resentment and resistance co-existed with a tradition of mutual expectations and reciprocal responsibilities that Eugene Genovese, in his *Roll, Jordan, Roll* (1976), calls "paternalism." This paternalistic ethos, widely accepted by the planters, was succinctly stated by antebellum Mississippian E. N. Elliott, himself a planter, who wrote that "Slavery is the duty and obligation of the slave to labor for the benefit of both master and slave, under a warrant to the slave of protection, and a comfortable subsistence...." Elliott placed great stress on the *rights* of the slave, not only the right of protection and subsistence, but of "counsel and guidance ... of care and attention in sickness and old age." [1] There were, no doubt, planters who fell short, even woefully short, of this standard, but the paternalist idea (leavened by Christian influence) was deeply internalized by the planters; it was, for most of them, the cornerstone of their self-respect.

Consider some of the ways in which blacks and whites interacted in the plantation household, whether under the demands of mutual obligation or by the simple exigencies of daily life. The middling sort of plantation—those having less than 50 slaves and not more than a thousand acres under cultivation—were predominant. But aside from the smallest yeoman plantations, most were like little self-sufficient villages in which the races mingled unceasingly. At the center was the "big house," of course, and surrounding it in close proximity were numerous other structures: barns, smokehouses, carriage houses, various kinds of storage facilities and workshops, mills, slaughter houses and slave quarters—these latter almost always within sight of the big house. Hardly an hour of the master's day would pass without some dealings with slaves or "servants," as they were usually called—at the breakfast table, in dealing with slave disputes or requests, in riding his fields to ensure that the work was proceeding properly or to inspect livestock, in the evenings at meals, or at his leisure, which might take many forms, most of which entailed the presence or the active involvement of slaves. This was especially true of hunting and fishing, usually male activities and almost always involving both masters and salves, young and old. And it is likely that this same master was in infancy nursed by a slave, just as his own children would be nursed—perhaps by the same slave woman or her daughter, since these roles were often passed down. Indeed, slave children and white children were often nursed together. One slave, Mattie Logan, recalled that she was born about the same time as her mistress's daughter, Jennie: "They say that I nursed on one breast while that white child ... pulled away at the other!" (see Genovese's *Plantation Household*). Visiting Northerners were often shocked by this sort of thing, needless to say.

---

1 The quotes are from Elliott's introduction to *Cotton is King*, an anthology of proslavery writings published in 1860. It can be accessed online at Project Gutenberg.

As for the mistress of the plantation household, if anything she was even more deeply involved in the lives of the servants. While she did not typically work in the kitchen alongside her black cook, she supervised the menus, managed the kitchen garden, and generally kept watch over all household activities related to the woman's sphere. Providing for the clothing of the slaves, sometimes a huge job, fell within that sphere, so her duties included the management of all spinning, weaving and dying, some of which she was adept at herself, but most of which involved skilled slave women. She was expected, as well, to attend to the health of the slaves, to visit the sick in the slave quarters and to ensure their proper medical care. In the event of a slave death, it was her duty to arrange proper burial. The diaries and narratives attest frequently to the sincere grief that many masters and mistresses felt over the deaths of trusted and beloved servants, some of which may well have been their playmates when they were children.

Finally, before moving on to the period following the War, I must note the shared traditions of worship on the plantation. The literature on this issue is quite complex. Early on, prior to the Revolution, masters appear to have been largely indifferent about the beliefs and religious practices of their slaves (and in the 18th century, it must be noted, fervent religious practice was not habitual among the planters themselves). With the advent of the 19th century and the growing influence of evangelical religion (propagated especially by Baptist and Methodist preachers / missionaries), the large numbers of slave conversions to Christianity appear to have been mostly sincere. The planters were not untouched by those same currents. Many pious masters provided for chapels on the plantation grounds, encouraged slave worship, and in some cases even presided over worship, including daily worship. After the Nat Turner and Stono uprisings, the planters became especially attentive to the spiritual needs of their slaves, believing that Christian influence, properly supervised, would help to prevent further disturbances of that kind. In any case, mutual participation in worship was common, and some slave preachers were popular not only with slave congregants but with the planters, too.

After Appomattox, everything changed, and yet in a certain sense much stayed the same. Initially, many of the freedmen were reluctant to return to the plantations, even as wage laborers, but other economic opportunities were scarce. Some, it's true, were able to purchase confiscated land for very low prices, as was the case in parts of the Lowcountry, especially in the Sea Islands—properties which became known as "heir's properties." Many did eventually return to the land as wage laborers, and many others eventually found a place, all over the South, as sharecroppers and tenant farmers in the crop-lien system, which gave them (along with poor whites) at least the semblance of economic independence. But despite such changes the integration of black and white cultures remained the norm in the rural areas and, to a lesser extent, in the towns, though it is true that some *voluntary* segregation occurred, most notably in the churches.

However, it is at this point that I must briefly review the central controversy in the history of the segregation story prior to the emergence of the Jim Crow regime in the early 1890s. In *The Strange Career of Jim Crow*, C. Van Woodward had argued (in the first edition of that work, pub. in 1955) that when segregation did appear during Reconstruction, it was with a few exceptions voluntary, and even then not extensive enough to justify any attempt to "equate this period in racial relations with *either* the old regime of slavery *or* with the future rule of Jim Crow." The old antebellum paternalism did not dissolve overnight, though it was often strained. Of course, one of the aims of the Radical Republicans was to achieve both political equality and social integration, and we can allow that segregation *might* have accelerated more rapidly prior to the rise of the Redeemers had not Republican dominance enforced some degree of integration. Yet even under Reconstruction rule, some forms of segregation appeared without interference from the Republicans—for example, public school segregation in North Carolina has been well-documented.

Joel Williamson, in his *After Slavery: The Negro in SC During Reconstruction* (1965), challenges Woodward's argument at some length, concluding that during Reconstruction "segregation had [already] crystallized into a comprehensive pattern." Williamson makes much of the few cases of documented non-voluntary segregation, and a good deal more of what he sees as a clear pattern of voluntary segregation. But he does so without properly contextualizing the frequent instances of mutual distrust that had emerged between the races at the War's end. For example, he quotes a traveler from Boston who, passing through Charleston in 1865, reported on the "growth of a bitter and hostile spirit between blacks and whites." Williamson cites a number of examples of such a hostile spirit, but leaves the impression that this hostility on the part of whites was a fundamentally irrational racism that had always been implicit in the ideology of white superiority, and which became uglier and more aggressive when blacks were no longer retrained by the yoke of slavery. Yet, in spite of all this, he admits that there is "no clear, concise answer to the question of why separation occurred...," while failing to give proper weight to the degree to which whites felt threatened by the Radical Republican regime. It is well to remember that this was a time when the northern armies had not yet withdrawn, when land confiscation (and the threat of widespread redistribution) was still an ongoing enterprise, and when state legislatures were dominated by radical Republicans—to say nothing of the daily frictions which occurred in the towns and cities when whites accustomed to obeisance were confronted by sometimes unruly and aggressive displays of social equality on the sidewalks and in public conveyances.

 This all seems to point toward a fairly "clear and concise" answer to Williamson's question. Under the circumstances it is hardly surprising that some degree of voluntary separation occurred during Reconstruction, though the measure of that distance is hard to ascertain. The circumstances varied a good deal from state to state, and hard evidence is sparse. Much of Williamson's argument relies on anecdotal evidence, a good deal of which has the appearance of cherry-picking, and he was focused almost exclusively on South Carolina. Nevertheless, he is not without the support of historians who lean toward his side in the debate. Responding to his critics in the 3rd edition of *Strange Career*, Woodward doesn't deny the existence of pockets of voluntary segregation, or, for that matter, some instances of enforced segregation, but rejects the notion that any substantial pattern of *proto*-Jim Crow segregation was already being established. Instead, he views the period as one full of "crosscurrents and contradictions, revolutionary innovations and violent reactions," within which the racial relations of "the old regime often persisted stubbornly into the new order...." In short, it was a period of instability that could not endure for long.

After 1877 the so-called Redeemers ushered in a new era of "Home Rule" but initially changed little in the realm of race relations. They did not seek to expand segregation in the sweeping fashion that would be typical of the Jim Crow regimes of the 1890s. On the contrary, they for the most part acquiesced, at least in the early years of their rule, to the reality of the black franchise and went out of their way to appeal to black voters. And what they offered the Freedmen can be summed up in a single word: *protection*. The Redeemers were transitional figures in a period fraught with political and economic hostility. At one extreme of the southern political spectrum was the rising power of the radical wing of the Democratic party—the faction of racial extremists—and at the other, the increasingly influential voices of the Populists (initially the Farmers Alliance), for whom the racial question was secondary to the message of class warfare that drew millions of small farmers to their ranks (both black and white). The Redeemers needed black votes to solidify their own vulnerable position, nor did many of them seem to have any stomach for a segregationist message that they associated with the white lower classes. Thus, the leading Redeemers sought to keep alive the old paternalism, to offer themselves to black voters as their protectors against the increasingly rancorous threat of the radical segregationists.

It may be the case that what Eugene Genovese calls a "residue of the old sense of duty" was more important than their political ambition, yet it should also be noted that large numbers of Redeemers were old Whigs in new wigs, so to speak, and were closely allied with the economic forces that would come to be associated with the New South: They sat on the boards of railroads (alongside their Yankee counterparts), as well as the boards of textile and steel enterprises (see Woodward's *Origins of the New South*) and generally saw the Populists, especially as the 1990s approached, as their *bête noire*. If it was necessary to compromise with the segregationists to maintain power against what was widely perceived as a "socialist" threat, so be it.

By the late 1880s the tide was beginning to turn and, in the midst of a major economic recession, the policies of the Redeemers were compromised, either by their own willingness to collude with the extremists, or by the growing power of the extremists as power brokers. (Even as early as 1877, it should be noted, even so venerated a figure as Wade Hampton won the governor's race in South Carolina only with the support of the infamous Ben Tillman, who by then already controlled a decisive bloc of Upcountry Democratic voters.) But there are other factors involved in the almost two decades of delay in the onslaught of Jim Crow legislation (which had begun in the late 1880s but did not really achieve a full head of steam until the middle years of the 1890s, especially after the 1896 *Plessy* v. *Ferguson* decision, which opened the legal door to "separate but equal" segregationist policies). While Woodward's critics saw plenty of evidence of continuity where he saw discontinuity, and while a good deal of their evidence is valid, Woodward's thesis remains relevant.

The Jim Crow era was not inevitable, and one overlooked factor in the sudden rush to *de jure* segregation is the issue of *class*. In an uncertain economic environment, many white voters, especially poor whites (but not exclusively so) feared black competition. It is difficult to disentangle deeply felt racial hatred from the fear that one's economic well-being or one's fragile class status might be imperiled. One thinks here of William Faulkner's memorable short story "Barn Burning," in which a white sharecropper of the 1880s, Abner Snopes, justifies his barn burning as an inchoate act of class warfare against the Bourbon whites. "I reckon I'll have a word with the man who aims to begin owning me tomorrow, body and soul," he says, just a few days before he burns his last barn. The owner of the barn in question is Colonel Sartoris, whose stately white mansion represents for Abner something built on "nigger sweat," and if he, Abner, is going to be exploited by that same landowner, it must mean that his own sweat will be of no greater value. In short, it is no real stretch to imagine that the radical segregationists were prepared to exploit such class resentments for their own purposes, and to make blacks convenient pawns in their game.

The fact is that black labor was essential to the rise of the New South, and blacks somehow had to be accommodated while white agrarian radicals were appeased. Blacks were increasingly disenfranchised by poll taxes, literacy tests, and other means, but there is some evidence that, among a segment of the black leadership, the segregation solution offered certain benefits. As Woodward had suggested and as Howard Rabinowitz argued at greater length in his "More than the Woodward Thesis: Assessing *the Strange Career of Jim Crow*" (1988),[2] the alternative to segregation (by the 1890s) appeared to be *exclusion*. The failed Black Codes of the late 1860s had been an attempt at exclusion, a partial restoration of the antebellum status quo, and from the point of view of the black leadership, this remained an undesirable possibility, especially in view of the retreat of northern Republicans from the goals of Reconstruction. The importance of this retreat, co-incident with the rise of the reconciliationist sentiment in both the North and the South, is a factor that can hardly be overstated. As Joel Williamson has argued at some length, northern Republican interest in black equality began to wane considerably after Reconstruction, and by the 1890s "politicians of both parties showed a disposition to use black people when they could and to abandon them when they could not."

Moreover, as a number of historians have noted, the North was quite familiar with segregation laws, since those laws had been pioneered in the North prior to the War, and some persisted well after. In most northern states during the colonial and antebellum eras, numerous local ordinances restricted the movements of free blacks, segregated them by occupation, relegated them to undesirable neighborhoods, and ensured separation in education. Some states in the Midwest and the West sought to exclude blacks entirely. After 1896 northern attitudes began to harden considerably, and even many of those who had most ardently supported the

---

2 *Journal of American History*, vol. 73, no. 3 (December 1988)

abolitionist cause looked with trepidation at the possibility of large numbers of poor blacks moving north, particularly since social and economic unrest among poor whites in the larger northern cities was at a critical stage. Hence, after the turn of the century, the North tacitly, and then quite openly, adopted a hands-off policy toward the South, allowing the proliferation of Jim Crow laws below the Mason-Dixon line, and, by various means, maintaining de facto segregation within their own states.

During the late 1890s and in the first decade of the new century, Jim Crow laws in the South, now with the support of both the radicals and the Conservatives, proliferated dramatically. Segregation became common in restaurants, waiting rooms, hospital wards, sports and sporting facilities, prisons, transportation, education, burial grounds, and in many other areas of southern life. Notoriously, even some courtrooms had Jim Crow Bibles for the swearing in of blacks (a reality that, some 20 years earlier, had been proposed in jest by an anti-segregationist wag writing for the Charleston *News and Courier*). All of this is the fodder of high school textbooks and I don't need to belabor it here.

However, I would like at this point to delve into two areas of concern that have not been so widely discussed or appreciated. The first of these involved the economics of what is called the "job-reservation system." Simply put, this means that under the Jim Crow regime economic exclusion was used to reinforce the segregation system by forcing blacks out of (or barring their entrance into) whole categories of occupations: white collar jobs, of course, but also various kinds of skilled labor and supervisory positions. This exclusion was not always written into law but often took the form of a widespread understanding among white employers. John W. Cell, in his *The Highest Stage of White Supremacy*, notes that "coercive mechanisms" were a "mixture of formal arrangements and informal understandings," and were pervasive. What is most interesting about this is that the job-reservation system, in effect, prevented whites "from behaving as rational economic persons ...," meaning that individual employers were unable to hire blacks for certain positions even when doing so would have made more economic sense, since blacks, even when their level of skill was equal to that of while workers in a given occupation, could always be paid less. The importance of this observation is that it brings us back to the issue of *class*, and to how the system of segregation was sometimes only superficially about race, per se, but just as importantly about the manipulation of the white labor force in an era when the South's economy had begun to rebound but was still trailing far behind the rest of the country in its productive capacity and standard of living. In short, the millions of blacks excluded from competing directly with whites in hundreds of occupations constituted what Cell calls a "reserve army of labor" and was thus "a potent weapon with which white workers could be threatened, intimidated and isolated." Needless, to say, under such conditions, labor unions made little headway in Dixie, and that remains largely true today.

The second concern I wish briefly to address is education, for in the long and strange tale of segregation, black education is perhaps the strangest part of the story. Prior to Reconstruction, few blacks in the South had any education at all, and most were simply illiterate (as were most poor whites). Under Reconstruction mandates, what few public schools there were, were integrated, and in some places like New Orleans, successfully so for more than a decade. With the arrival of the Redeemers the literacy rates were still dismal, but in the rush to industrialize, public schools were in greater demand. During the Jim Crow era, virtually all public schooling in the South was segregated, but black schools were hardly "equal," if the disproportionately low funding they were allocated is any indication. Yet many black leaders in the South remained optimistic about black education. They recognized that things could be worse and that many conservative white legislators across the South were at least making some effort to adhere to the letter of the "separate but equal" clause of *Plessy* v. *Ferguson*. Black leaders foresaw the possibility of gradual advancement and worked to improve what access they had to public schooling, and, of course, to found black colleges.

The most important of these leaders was Booker T. Washington, who had been born into slavery, and who established himself as the pre-eminent voice in the South for a philosophy of "gradualism," most memorably expressed in 1895 in his famous address known as the "Atlanta Compromise," focusing especially on black businesses and education. As early as 1881 he had established the Tuskegee Institute in Alabama for the primary purpose of training teachers who would then spread across the rural South to instruct black youths in the skills they needed for participating in the work force as skilled laborers, farmers, and tradesmen. Within a few years of the "Atlanta Compromise" speech, Washington's ideas and influence were routinely attacked by northern black activists such as W.E.B Dubois, who was one of the founders of the recently formed NAACP, which regarded Washington as an obstacle to racial equality. In their view, he was infinitely prolonging the march to full equality, while pandering to white elites in both the North and the South, and encouraging an attitude of quiescent acceptance of the status quo among the black masses.

This is the view of the "Wizard of Tuskegee" that prevails even today, and few Americans have any idea just how successful Washington and his followers were in improving the lot of blacks in the South. While much of the damage to his reputation is the result of the way he is caricatured in history textbooks or in the popular media, much can also be attributed to the scathing portrait of his philosophy offered up in Ralph Ellison's novel *Invisible Man*, a chapter of which is commonly anthologized in high school and college texts under the title "Battle Royal," where the philosophy of gradualism is brilliantly but unfairly mocked.

Yet well before the *Brown* v. *Board of Education* decision in 1954, which brought the era of school segregation to an end, Washington's disciples (he having died in late 1915) had done a great deal to build the character and effectiveness of black education in the South. Washington himself regarded segregation not chiefly as an obstacle to his goals but as an opportunity. Direct competition with whites, perhaps especially in the area of education, was premature. Separated from that debilitating arena, black children might thrive. And, indeed, there is evidence that in many cases across the South they did.

One of those who looked upon Washington's accomplishments with approval was Zora Neale Hurston, whom many would regard as among the greatest American writers of the 20th century. Hurston knew from direct experience (as a teacher and anthropologist) what a number of recent studies by black scholars such as Betty Jamerson Reed and Adam Fairclough have argued—that all-black schools (both public and private) in the segregation era had often been thriving centers of education and community involvement. [3]

Of course, the final irony in this strange tale is that today, well over half a century after the *Brown* decision, and despite any number of attempts to force the issue through social engineering, American public schools and American society in general, remain largely segregated, but less so in the South than elsewhere. Why this is so is another, quite complex story, but I might venture to say—by way of ending where I began—that it has something to do with the fact that in the South blacks and whites, despite many trials and tribulations, share a common identity that is not so prevalent in other regions of the county. Perhaps, too, it has something to do with the still dominant belief across the Christian South, in the saving power of forgiveness, as demonstrated so vividly by the outpouring of forgiveness and generosity that prevailed in the wake of the Emanuel church shooting on that terrible evening in June, 2015, here in Charleston, from whence I write.

---

[3] For a more detailed account of Hurston's views on the *Brown* decision and related matters, see the essay in this volume entitled "Zora Neale Hurston's White Mule."

GRACE KING AND THE PRAYERS OF WOMEN

Grace King died in New Orleans in 1932, the city where she was born and lived a long and productive life. Virtually all of her fictional works are set in that city or its outlying parishes, and she is generally associated with the "local-color" movement in American letters that emerged and flourished in the decades following the defeat of the Confederacy. To some extent this designation is correct. King, in common with most "local color" writers, focused on characters and settings that, to her largely metropolitan, northern readers, were decidedly exotic, far removed from the increasingly complex and standardized world of the Gilded Age.

Yet King's work transcends the limits of local color, which was all too often crafted opportunistically for audiences hungry for sentimental plots with little or no depth of characterization—all served up with a dollop of eccentricity. Like two other New Orleans writers of her period, George Washington Cable and Kate Chopin, King was among the pioneers of the psychological realism that we so often take for granted in the modern novel. True, as some of her critics have noted, there is an element of idealism in her treatment of the southern past. Unlike Cable, for instance, she was a staunch defender of the Confederate legacy and a trenchant critic of Reconstruction, wary of New South ideologues and their—in her view—unseemly eagerness to embrace the gospel of Progress. Yet in her best work there is also a thread of irony and ambivalence, a determined refusal to conceal the tragic fatality that eats away at our dreams of happiness. If her deeply flawed characters sometimes find reconciliation or consolation, it is always at a substantial price.

In King's deeply Christian moral universe, self-knowledge is possible, but remains a rare commodity, always elusive. In one of her early journal entries she writes,

> We do not know what we are—we cannot see ourselves, but we know what we might be. The loom works out a beautiful design, in its silk—The design strung up on the top of the loom—and told out line by line to the shuttle—and the woven piece is rolled up underneath—the loom cannot see that either; it recalls spots of it, here and there, by memory—it cannot compare the silk with the picture—the outsider must do it. We carry our pattern in our head—and weave our lives the best we can with our machinery—God only knows when the roll is finished how nicely we followed the pattern—Each one's life is a roll of goods in the warehouse of Eternity.

This passage, with its obliquely Shakespearean echo in the opening line, is at once a splendid image of divine Providence and a metaphor for the writer's art. Note the telling pun in the phrase "told out line by line." The verb "told," from the Middle English *tellen*, can mean both to count and to narrate. Like God, the storyteller—the "outsider"—deals in destinies, and knows better than most how essentially blind to its own destiny is each human heart. But it is also suggestive that this extended metaphor's "vehicle" is a traditionally feminine tool—the loom. For King, women are the most natural storytellers, and much of her work is derived from the many stories that she first heard told by other women—her grandmother, her own mother, and many others.

Indeed, in the prologue to her most accomplished collection of short fiction, *Balcony Stories* (1892), King pays homage to those southern women who "love to sit and talk together of summer nights, on balconies, in their vague, loose white garments ... their sleeping children within easy hearing," who in their "soft mother-voices" talk about this person and that, "old times, old friends, old experiences; and it seems to them that there is no end ... of the mother knowledge." They speak especially of the lives of other women, of their "destinies ... what God has done or is doing with other women whom they have known." Each story, she writes, "has some unique and peculiar pathos [which the teller] dramatizes and inflects, trying to make the point, visible to her, apparent [also] to her listeners." And as the women murmur their tales in soft voices so as not to wake sleeping children just behind half open shutters, one of those children lies awake nonetheless, gazing across the "dim forms on the balcony," making "stores for the future...." King's authorial voice, then, is an extension and a fusion of many female voices, and at times it is impossible to know which of her tales is the product of her own invention and which the offspring of memory. Perhaps it would be safest to say that many or most of them are a compound of both.

Tales of mothers and daughters are among the staples of King's art, but one of her most poignant, also her first published story, "Monsieur Motte," concerns a motherless daughter—an orphan, in fact—whose papa died in the War and whose mother passed away just a few years after her birth, leaving the four-year-old Marie Modeste in the care of a quadroon, a family servant and hairdresser, Marcelite. When the story opens Marie is 17 and has been a year-round boarding student for 13 years at the Institute of St. Denis—a school for the daughters of the Creole elite. For all of those years Marcelite has visited St. Denis almost every day—she is the school's hairdresser, as well—to care for Marie's material needs—her clothes, her *toilette*, and her hair. For the quadroon, a middle-aged, portly woman, Marie is more than a material care; in her "maternal" heart she regards the girl as virtually her own daughter, but the color line prevents her from outwardly crossing over into that role. Yet it is apparent that the girl has become the focal point of Marcelite's life, a passion which at times spills over into abject adoration. When she dresses Marie on the afternoon of the year's most anticipated social event, *The Grande Concert Musicale*, which will be followed by a graduation commencement, she gazes upon the girl with "desperate … caressing eyes." Producing from a wrapped box a pair of exquisitely crafted boots, Marcelite takes Marie's "white foot … in her dark palm," kissing it "over and over again" and nestling it "in her bosom" while talking "babytalk to it in Creole." Placing the first of the new shoes upon the fragile foot, she takes pains to ensure that its "glossy white should meet with no defilement."

Passages like this, presented without a trace of King's more characteristic irony, suggest why modern critics have not embraced her work with quite the same fervent enthusiasm reserved for King's contemporary, Kate Chopin. Well-versed in the myriad nuances of white supremacy, many readers today will be inclined to see in Marcelite's unquestioning acceptance of her own inferiority a flagrant instance of how racist assumptions were internalized by the objects of white prejudice. We are inclined to demand some sign—a hint, at least—of authorial disapproval. But King offers no such sign. On the contrary she has the bad taste to parade this scene before us as if it were perfectly acceptable! As if the self-sacrificial devotion of a half-caste woman of color for a lily-white Creole orphan could be taken at face value, as if it were not somehow degrading for people of color everywhere!

There is, one suspects, at least an implied defiance in King's portrait of Marcelite's relationship with Marie Modeste. To some extent it can be read as a reposte to George Washington Cable, the New Orleans novelist whose *Old Creole Days* (1879) was still all the rage in the literary world. Cable had depicted the Creole culture in a decidedly negative light, as a culture corrupted by racial pride. King made it known on more than one occasion that she felt Cable "had stabbed [New Orleans] in the back …" to pacify northern sensibilities on the racial issue. King, who was no Creole, but educated in Creole schools and immersed in Creole culture, seems to insist in this story and elsewhere, that relations across the color line were far more generous than a writer like Cable would allow. It is true that King never seriously questions the racial hierarchy, but her stories reveal in numerous instances that blacks could be, and frequently were, *morally* superior to whites; but in one journal entry King criticizes Cable for upholding standards of morality that grant the highest virtues *only* to blacks, leaving moral "degradation" for whites. In her own work, virtue and vice are color blind.

Yet what is most interesting about King's first published story, and what drives its plot, is the mystery of its titular persona—the long-awaited Monsieur Motte who never appears. To Marie, he is a faceless uncle who has financed her education and all her needs through his intermediary, Marcelite; to Marie's schoolmates, her teachers, and even St. Denis' headmistress, he is a half-mythical and reclusive Creole aristocrat whose constant generosity has given Marie a certain *cachet* at the school. He is the guarantor of her eventual glittering debut in Creole society, a debut which is Marie's fondest hope. But his existence is all a lie, a fiction that Marcelite has maintained for 13 years with an endless stream of excuses for his failure to visit his niece. Now, when the moment has arrived, when Marie is about to cross the threshold into womanhood, Marcelite is faced with the ordeal of revealing the truth that will surely crush the expectant girl. Monsieur Motte is purely a creature of Marcelite's pity for her orphan charge. The clothes, the candies, the stories of his eccentric ways, even Marie's tuition—all were Marcelite's own doing, all the result of her unflagging but misguided devotion to the fragile white girl whose only real protector in the world is a corpulent quadroon.

In the end, Marie never learns the truth, and it is Marcelite who suffers most profoundly from her deceit. In part this is because her own hopes are crushed. In her own imagination, too, Monsieur Motte had taken on life, had become a second self. Now, she was merely Marcelite, the faithful servant. "Her brave personation was over." As Monsieur Motte, "what could she not do? If only she could have created him out of her own death! If only she could have made what she so happily invented!"

Thwarted hopes are a frequent theme in King's stories, especially the thwarted hopes of women. "Disappointment cracks us all—us women," remarks the Head Mistress in "Monsieur Motte." She adds, "I am sure we are all cracked somewhere; the fracture may be hidden, but never mind, it is there, and every woman knows just where it is, and feels it too." In another of the *Balcony Stories*,

"A Crippled Hope," a slave child, permanently deformed after her mother dropped her as a baby, lives for years in a slave trader's mart in the days prior to the War, utterly ignorant of the outside world, her feckless mother having long since been sold, leaving "little Mammy" (as she is called) alone. Her sole hope is that one day a kind Master or Mistress will buy her and give her a home. But her hope is an illusion because the slave trader under whom she toils values her too much as a nurse to the often-ailing slaves who pass through the mart. So reduced is the scope of her existence that, when the War comes, she knows nothing of it, and is bewildered suddenly to find herself a free woman, left to her own devices. Yet she cares nothing for freedom; she feeds only upon her old hope of finding a Mistress. She wanders a ruined countryside, nursing the sick and the maimed, for she had an understanding "of the mysteries of the flesh." But this vocation is of little consolation to her. She grieves over the mystery of providence, for it seems to her that, just as her mother had done, "God had let her drop."

Similarly, in "The Story of a Day," an Acadian girl of tender years dreams of her impending marriage to a young man of the bayou. Adorine longs with an almost mystical rapture for that moment when she will become a mother, and then a grandmother, surrounded by a numerous brood of loving children and grandchildren. But on her wedding day, her young fiancé meets with a mysterious death in the bayou as he makes his way by pirogue over the treacherous waters. Now Adorine lives out her days at her spinning wheel in an "unfaltering" refusal to be consoled, wearing her hair in the same glossy black ringlets that she had worn as she awaited the arrival of her lost lover. This story, which reads like a dark parable or fairy tale, is nonetheless rich in realistic detail and psychological penetration. The narrator speaks with a woman's inflection of Adorine's fate, in a voice that steadfastly refuses to offer the reader any cheap comfort, just as Adorine refuses herself that comfort. But there is a transcendence in this refusal, and in the deep current of sympathy that suffuses the telling.

Perhaps the most memorable story in this vein, and certainly the most stylistically innovative, is "Madrilene: Or, the Festival of the Dead," which first appeared in *Harper's Magazine* in 1890.

Set on the eve of All Saints, "Madrilene" begins with omniscient narration, then almost seamlessly slips into limited omniscience until, finally, the narrative voice all but disappears in a frantic *babble* of voices that at moments anticipates the high modernist technique of writers like James Joyce or Ford Maddox Ford. The protagonist, Madrilene, is a supposed quadroon of 15, who lives in a "colored" bordello run by Madame Lais (a name perhaps derived from the famous courtesan of ancient Greece), whose family of half-caste "daughters," as she calls them, cater to the needs of affluent white men. Madrilene, who has steadfastly resisted Madame Lais' attempts to prostitute her, earns her room and board as a household drudge.

Free to come and go as she pleases when her work is done, she spends much of her time haunting a nearby cemetery—almost certainly the St. Louis Cemetery #2, built in 1823. This is, of course, one of New Orleans' most legendary Cities of the Dead, one in which all the vaults, or "ovens," are stacked above ground like "mortuary hotels," as King calls them. There, Madrilene finds refuge from the poverty and misery of her life. There, too, under the tutelage of the cemetery's sexton, an ancient and alcoholic Creole, she has secretly learned to read. The central conflict in the story emerges when, on the eve of All Saints, Madrilene throttles a performing monkey on the street just outside the cemetery gates and slaps its owner, a quadroon boy, for allowing the monkey to attack a passing white child. Neither boy nor monkey is seriously harmed, but when word of the incident gets back to the boy's mother, a virago by the name of Palmyre, the stage is set for a violent encounter later that night which will lead to Madrilene's apparent death.

King's biographer, Robert Bush, has called this story a "macabre melodrama" and clearly doesn't regard it as among her best, for it is omitted from his anthology of her work, *Grace King of New Orleans*. The story *has* been taken more seriously by a few of King's feminist critics, but in a manner which fundamentally distorts its meaning. The best example of this is Clara Juncker's essay "Grace King: Woman as Artist."[1] Juncker zealously ferrets through every

---

[1] *The Southern Literary Journal,* vol. 20, no. 1 (Fall 1987), pp. 37-44.

nook and cranny of the tale looking for evidence that King's deepest intention there was to allegorize the "birthpangs of the woman writer," who struggles to articulate a "new text of Semiotic desire." According to Juncker, women writers of King's era were relegated to "linguistic marginality, ... enclosed in masculine sign systems." At the climax of the tale, when Madrilene is attacked and stabbed by the demonic Palmyre on the threshold of Madame Lais' brothel, we are to understand, writes Juncker, that Madrilene's pain and degradation are "authored by the Phallus, the cutting knife which threatens her very existence.... But it is precisely [her] struggle against the Phallic weapon that engenders her creativity."

One might well wonder how a knife wielded by a hysterical female quadroon can be transformed into a symbol of phallic oppression, but in the realm of much feminist criticism, this is par for the course. Had the knife been a backscratcher and the wielder a trained seal, the conclusion would have been the same. Grace King has not been well served by her critics. But Juncker is correct about one thing, "Madrilene" *is* an allegory, but not an allegory of the sort she imagines. Indeed, the evidence is lying around right out in the open, and it is astonishing that no one has bothered to notice.

Madrilene is short for Marie Madeleine, the French variant of Mary Magdalen. This is stressed at least half a dozen times in the story, particularly when Madrilene is addressed by the old priest and sexton, who refuses to use the "vulgar" contraction. It is true that the name is not uncommon in French communities, but in this case the name is pointedly associated with prostitution, just as the name of Mary Magdalen was (though falsely) in medieval iconography. Madrilene is not a prostitute, but she dwells in a house of ill repute, and is tainted by that association. In the iconographic tradition, there are certain features in the depiction of Mary Magdalen that recur. According to legend, Magdalen, a penitential figure, is supposed to have withdrawn to a cave in the wilderness after the death of Christ, there to pray for her soul and the souls of the dead. Thus, she is depicted by Donatello, in his sculpture in the Florence Baptistry, as a painfully thin image of suffering, with dark, sunken eyes. In fact, the outlines of the skull beneath her face suggest the very image of death. Her lips are parted ecstatically in prayer and her eyes gaze out upon vacancy, as if she were contemplating the prospect of paradise.

To a significant extent this image of Donatello's Magdalen is very much a part of the tradition of his predecessors' depictions. Magdalen's hair is usually fashioned as long and flowing, and almost always as unkempt and tangled. In addition, she is frequently portrayed kneeling and weeping before a tomb (recalling her role as the first to discover the disappearance of her savior after the Resurrection), sometimes naked (though covered by her hair), and often clothed in a coarse garment or skin, signifying mortification. In a study of the Magdalen iconography, Bess Bradfield notes the saint is revealed as "one whose body is being thoroughly threshed by suffering in order to enter paradise undefiled." In Donatello's Magdalen, the body is show as "being stripped of all former meaning." In short, Magdalen is depicted as one who has chosen to enter Purgatory while still in this life.

With the exception of the long and flowing hair, all of these attributes are associated with King's Madrilene, as well. Upon her first appearance we are told that she is tall and emaciated, and that her face, "though young, seemed created to be overshadowed by the emblems of death: a thin skin ... hollow eyes, brooding brows, and ... eyes fixed in studied abstraction." The upper half of her body is covered by a "shrunken sacque"—the term "sacque" deriving ultimately from the Greek *sakkos*, a bag made out of coarse cloth or hair. When Madrilene is described in greater detail a little later in the story, the "unfleshed cheekbone" is again stressed. Her skin is bruised, her eye-sockets are "opaque" "dry" and "burned out"—as if to suggest the depths of her suffering. And the eyes themselves, in one of the most striking passages in the tale, are "black and disturbed, not with hidden conflicts and rebellions, but carrying, like godless worlds, their unshaped contents in chaos." Added to this is her hair, short but "ill-kept." When she visits the tomb of the woman she falsely believes to be her mother, Madrilene brings as a gift to the dead one a beaded medallion depicting a "weeping figure" before a tomb. This sort of medallion is mentioned twice in the story, and apparently the image of the weeping figure, so reminiscent of Mary Magdalen, was commonly embossed upon trinkets sold during All Saints festivities.

Most importantly, as these iconographic parallels already suggest, Madrilene is associated with suffering, death and resurrection. And each of these themes is an integral aspect of the Festival of the Dead, a purgatorial feast when the tombs of the dead are cleansed and prayers for the dead are intoned. A frequent motif in such prayers is that of the "gates of Paradise" through which, it is fervently hoped, the souls of those suffering purgatorial flames will soon pass. For Madrilene, the gates which lead into the St. Louis cemetery are a foretaste of Paradise. She is at home only when she passes through the cemetery gates, and, in clandestine fashion, gazes longingly at the interment of the dead, identifying with their trials, rejoicing with them as their souls are stripped of the fleshly encumbrance of the body's prison and rise to meet their Savior.

Perhaps it is this longing for death and resurrection that Robert Bush regards as "macabre." For Madrilene, the sexton, the one person to whom she could "lay bare her mind," is, despite his drunkenness, a figure of hope. He is the gatekeeper, the keeper of the keys to the gate of Paradise. On the night of her death, she attempts to seek refuge in the cemetery one last time, but for reasons that remain a mystery, the sexton does not appear, as is his custom, to unlock the gates. She is thus driven to seek refuge at the house of Madame Lais, whose gate may be understood in this context as the gate of Hell. It is there that Madrilene is attacked by the enraged Palmyre, stripped of her *sacque*, and dies, but not before she envisions herself rising above the demonic fury of this world, ascending "far, far above them all, where ... white forms were waiting for her as if she, too, were white." Part of the pathos of this tale is that Madrilene believes herself to be "colored," and associates the miracle of resurrection with the purity of whiteness. The final irony is that, as she gasps her last breath, her patrimony as a white child, daughter of a white father who mysteriously died in Madame Lais' brothel, is revealed. In short, the tale of Madrilene is an allegory of the soul's hope of resurrection. Madrilene, like each of us, is an outcast in a fallen world, mired in its black dross but longing for a paradisal purity that is ever elusive yet somehow foretold in the desire itself.

King's religious convictions are something of an enigma. She was by formal (and family) affiliation a Presbyterian, but her fiction is steeped in Catholic imagery. That her faith was real, there is no question. Her journals are filled with references to God, to churchgoing, and to prayer, and in one or two passages there is evidence of a powerful nature mysticism. In one journal entry, though, there is a cryptic passage in which she admits that, for three years prior to her mother's death, she did not attend services. She gives no reason, except to say that the cause was something that she could not speak about "even in these pages." Whether the cause was a personal matter or a crisis of faith is not clear, but there are hints that her faith did not always come easy, and that it rested in part upon her devotion to her beloved mother. Her fiction frequently alludes to the special relationship that God has with women, an intimate, intuitive relationship often absent in the more abstract faith of men, yet one which, at times, may tempt women to presume that God—like an imperious husband, or father, or master—needs to be gently led toward mercy, as though, lacking the mother-wisdom of women, God in his masculine self-absorption might stumble into cruelty or injustice without altogether meaning to.

This feminine presumption is evidently the point of "A Quarrel with God," one of the uncollected tales, first published in *Outlook* magazine in 1897. The story unfolds in the course of an afternoon at the nursing home of Madame B. in New Orleans. But Madame's B's establishment is unique; it is a home for indigent Confederate widows of good family, ladies whose misfortunes in the devastating aftermath of the War have led them by degrees into genteel poverty, whose family pride would never allow them to accept "charity." Madame B, a lady of similar social status, has arranged matters so that they are kept alive, but are given no more than the bare necessities, "nothing more than those necessities which ladies can offer and accept with honor." Among the old ladies in Madame B's home is Mademoiselle Herminie, the most prideful of them all, one whose shocking impieties have been the gist of their daily gossip.

As the story opens, M. Herminie lies on her deathbed and the focal point of the story's suspense is whether she will renounce an old quarrel with God, and seek forgiveness in her final moments.

Robert Bush admires this tale but complains that Herminie's reconciliation with God in the end is too pat, that the story would have been more interesting if King had allowed her to go one 'final round' with God, as it were, before allowing her to capitulate. Again, Bush misses the point. In "A Quarrel with God" Herminie's impiety and the possibility of a deathbed conversion is really little more than a pretext for King's satire. The most important figure in this tale is not Herminie but the ex-slave Florestine, Madame's B's assistant. It is Florestine who summons a priest to Herminie's bedside, and it is she who is given a monologue that runs on for almost five pages, dominating the second half of the story. Unhappy that the only priest that she could find at short notice is a "poor, humble, ignorant French priest—the servitor of one of the poorest parishes in the city," Florestine stations herself behind him as he makes his deathwatch, waiting for an opportunity to give the last rites to Herminie, who is presently unconscious. Florestine is certain that this poor priest is only good for "butcher people" and negroes, that he can't possibly understand the life of a woman of so noble a family as Herminie's. Florestine, with all the pride of a slave who once served one of the greatest families of the old regime, knows better.

King allows us to hear her thoughts before she begins to speak: "The Master must be informed! This was the summary of the subject in her mind. A soul in her institution was not to be damned, any more than in old times a slave on her plantation was to be whipped, without some attempt on her part for mercy." What is apparent is that Florestine intends to plant a few germane suggestions in the priest's ear, but it is not really the priest to whom she will speak, but to the Master, to God himself, who may, we can surmise, like the priest, need a little counseling on how to deal properly with the high and mighty. The priest is just a stand-in in this scene; in fact, he never opens his mouth.

Thus, Florestine begins to whisper in the priest's ear, all the while keeping a watchful eye on M. Herminie. Florestine's concern is that Herminie will need special handling if she is to be persuaded to repent of her quarrel. If she is proud, it is with good reason! Her grandfather, the old Colonel, was a "big man in the state," and even the governor used to tremble before him. He was "not afraid of God on His throne." But her own father was bigger still with "His balls and his dinners, and his fine cooking and his fine servants. His niggers were too fine to go [about] with other niggers! They had no use for God; their master was God in their eyes." Florestine implies that Herminie, descended of proud men, could hardly be other than proud herself. How can she be blamed for that? "God," she concedes, "is the master: [Herminie] must beg His pardon—[but] for what? Did she ever do anything? No, God in Heaven knows she never did anything against Him. And what? For a few words get a whipping?"

Again, she gives the deity His formal due: "God is right; the Master is always right; he owns his people and he's right to do what he pleases with them." And then, having hedged her bets, she plunges in deeper: "But the Master doesn't know *everything* that passes on his plantation, and ... if God ... knew what I know, He would not be so hard on M. Herminie." After all, the poverty of the rich is much harder than the poverty of the poor, who have known nothing else. And to be left alone, as she has been! "Listen, mon pere, do you know what it is to be left alone ... with nobody in this world to be your family? Well God did that to Herminie ...," leaving her with no one to love, "no one to sacrifice herself for." And that was not the worst of the things that God did to Herminie. Florestine leans closer to the priest, whispering almost inaudibly: "Do you know how her mother died?... It was in the family.... How can God create gentlemen so bad?" The implication is that Herminie's father contracted syphilis, then infected his wife, who slowly wasted away.

Having insinuated several times in the course of her monologue that the real scandal in this story is not Herminie's impiety but God's injustice—or, perhaps, simply His absent-mindedness—Florestine proceeds to her peroration: "Ah, mon pere, you are good, you are patient.... That is why I sent for you.... She is opening her eyes. Say something to her! Do not look at her! Do not listen to her! She is out of her head!... She does not know what she is about. Think of your mother, mon pere, and do your duty! God will understand...." It is true, she admits, that Herminie was proud, that she was cross and bad-tempered. "She was not like the other old ladies who sit there day after day with the patience and resignation of angels. If you choose," she says, "to call M. Herminie a sinner.... I will say yes."

But the implication is clear. If the priest, or, rather, God, chooses to brand Herminie a sinner, He will do so in dereliction of His duty. For Herminie is "out of her head." At that moment, Herminie awakes. As the narrator informs us, she opens her eyes. She performs her religious duty and dies at "peace with the world or God—whichever she had been at war with." So impatiently dismissive of this final act of repentance is King's narrator, that we have little choice but to conclude that it is not, after all, Herminie's quarrel with her maker that is of chief concern here. The priest assumes, based upon long experience, that the soul, after a long bout of suffering followed by a sudden waning of its pain just before death, emerges from that ordeal purged of all recrimination, childlike in its readiness to seek reconciliation. "Always the priest had found it was the women who had been most sorely tried ... who forgive most easily."

But the narrator offers us a choice. It "may have been according to Florestine's ... experience ... that the master would sometimes listen to an overheard explanation when he would not to a direct one; and one of her most successful devices as an advocate for mercy when a fellow-slave was in peril of punishment was to tell his story, as she knew how to tell such stories, just inside the master's hearing." Again, we are asked to consider the efficacious power of storytelling, of women's stories, to heal and to reconcile, like prayers. Perhaps King would have us understand that there is nothing, really, to choose. Both the priest and Florestine can lay claim to a part of the truth, a truth which raises but leaves unresolved the question of God's mercy. Certainly, King gently chides Florestine for her presumption. God is not, after all, a plantation master. But perhaps he is willing to grant the prayers of women, even presumptuous prayers, a privileged place in the providential order, if only to compensate women for the ingratitude of men.

THE FACES OF MEN

This year marks the sixtieth anniversary of the publication of Calder Willingham's novel *End as a Man* (1947), though chances are that most readers today have never heard of the book. Despite the accolades that it received from such leading literary lights of the immediate post-World War II era as James T. Farrell (who called it "a permanent contribution to American literature"), *End as a Man* now gathers dust on library bookshelves and remains largely unnoticed in studies of American fiction. Reasons for the neglect of this distinguished novel are not hard to find. One is that Willingham (born Calder Baynard Willingham, Jr., in Atlanta, in 1922) was only twenty-three when he wrote it, and it is not without its purple passages. A more telling reason, however, is that Willingham explores in the novel a theme that is virtually guaranteed to affront our epicene guardians of contemporary literary propriety: manhood.

End as a Man is set in a military college in the South, and explores a year (or something less than a year) in the lives of a group of cadets in the early 1940s. This fictional institution, called The Academy, is clearly modeled on The Citadel, which Willingham attended in 1940-41, before transferring to the University of Virginia. Several of these cadets are first-year "knobs" (as they are traditionally called because of their closely shaved heads), and much of the narrative is concerned with their efforts to cope with the school's rigorous discipline and the frequent hazing imposed upon them by upperclassmen. Freshman cadets in these pages are routinely braced, dressed down, forced to eat at attention, humiliated for betraying signs of weakness, and ridiculed for any peculiarity of appearance, speech, or manner. So prominent are these episodes, especially in the first half of the novel, that many readers have assumed that Willingham's chief concern was to demonstrate the cruelty of such a system of discipline. Alex Macaulay, for example, in a short article in the *New Georgia Encyclopedia*, summarizes *End as a Man* as a "scathing and lurid assessment of the overblown machismo that Willingham encountered at the Citadel." But this is far from the truth. To be sure, there are instances of "overblown machismo" on display, but, for the most part, Willingham presents hazing as a routine and highly ritualized fact of life at The Academy. No tender psyches are destroyed by the process, and, with one notable exception, the upperclassmen understand that the hazing ritual is strictly defined; they know when to relent, and when they forget, others remind them.

The most conspicuously "overblown machismo" in *End as a Man* belongs to one of the novel's chief characters, upperclassman Jocko de Paris, a cadet who has barely escaped expulsion on more than one occasion due to the intervention of his wealthy father, one of The Academy's most generous benefactors. De Paris is vividly presented as an isolated sadist, one for whom the hazing ritual is not an impersonal matter of discipline, but a brutal quest for personal satisfaction of desires that—so Willingham hints—arise out of a repressed homosexuality. He frequently violates the limits that his fellow upperclassmen observe, and the primary victim of de Paris' sadism is Maurice Simmons, a freshman cadet almost universally despised for his Ohio accent, red cabbage ears, and religious mania. On one occasion, de Paris salaciously accuses Simmons of having committed incestuous acts with his mother and sister, then beats his buttocks mercilessly with a broom until they are covered in blood. Yet there is no suggestion in Willingham's treatment of this or similar episodes that de Paris' abuse of the hazing system is to be understood as a condemnation of the system itself.

While *End as a Man* cannot be considered a novel of social protest in the vein of the naturalistic revival of the 1930s, it does share some traits with those novels. The tone is, throughout, one of almost clinical detachment, and while the narrative does feature a central character, freshman cadet Robert Marquales, he is in no sense a "hero." In fact, Willingham goes out of his way to prevent the reader from forming any bond of sympathy with Marquales. For well over a hundred pages, Marquales wanders passively from one encounter to the next, unable to find a place for himself, and irritably alienating his follow knobs. He is cruel to the hapless Simmons, is not particularly conscientious about his studies, and, worst of all, is so insecure that he foolishly allows himself to be drawn into an association with two disreputable upperclassmen. One of these is de Paris; the other is Perrin McKee, the vain, sickly, and homosexual son of an impoverished old family who is at once the most contemptible and yet the most fully realized character in the novel. McKee represents another, even more perverse image of manhood, one in revolt against the rank fecundity of the female body.

In a pompous speech delivered to his fellow cadets one evening in the barracks, McKee theorizes that the "true man" is he who has most completely integrated the "sub-experiential" aspect of his personality into conscious awareness, and proceeds to tell of how, when he was an infant, his mother passed him along to a "negress" wet nurse. "I sucked her black tits for eighteen months," McKee recalls. "[D]aily, I kneaded that glistening carbon flesh in my fat little hands [and] swallowed the thick yellow product of the Negress' blood...." But this "sub-experiential" memory was not recovered until years later when, still a boy, he witnessed a cousin of his being nursed at the breast of the same black woman. He was "repelled" by the sucking of those "little pink jaws" on the "monstrous organ." The thought that he had once done the same "plunged [him] into an illness of weeks." To cure him of this affliction, McKee's father forced him to watch "the little greedy cousin suck," and it is to this experience that McKee proudly attributes the "beginning of [his] intellectuality." Willingham implies that McKee's "intellectuality" (given by turns to grotesque abstraction and lurid flights of gothic fancy) is in fact a craven intellectual retreat from genuine manhood.

    While McKee does not quite speak openly of his homosexuality, it is clear that he regards that condition as proof of his own superiority. Indeed, when Marquales comes by accident into possession of a letter that McKee has anonymously addressed to Jocko de Paris, we learn the full extent of McKee's depravity. In the course of that letter (which is clearly intended to blackmail de Paris in return for sexual favors, but I will omit the sordid details), he theorizes at some length upon the evolutionary destiny of the "man not tolerant of woman." Heretofore, he argues, human development has been hampered by its dependence upon natural generation. But with the advent of "artificial propagation," all that will change. While in the past those "men intolerant of women" have been hounded and persecuted and unable, for the most part, to pass along the "power of their mutation," they will in the future become "more and more numerous." He envisions the evolutionary "demise" of the female and the emergence of a "virile, new man." In short, McKee imagines himself the forerunner of a superior new race destined to "people the earth like mountainous spore explosions with their own kind." Although Willingham clearly intends this sophomoric theorizing of McKee's to be read as a parody of Nietzschean naturalism, it also identifies McKee as the masochistic counterpart to the brutally sadistic de Paris. Indeed, McKee worships de Paris as a sort of Nietzschean *Übermensch*. In the moral economy of Willingham's novel, both of these cadets represent equally repulsive versions of masculinity.

    One of the weaknesses of *End as a Man* is that cadet Marquales' association with these two negative models of manhood is merely adventitious. While he is gratified by the signs of favor that they show him, he is not deeply drawn by or attracted to either. One could imagine a different novel in which Marquales, uncertain of his own masculinity, struggles in heroic fashion against the influence of both these models toward a more mature and genuinely virile understanding of manhood. But no such development arises. It is true that, in the end, he rejects the friendship of both, but only in a desperate attempt to save his own skin.

If there is a hero in this novel, it is the Academy's president, General A. L. Draughton, who emerges somewhat surprisingly at the end as the most admirable image of manhood on offer here. Early in these pages, Draughton (possibly modeled on General Charles P. Summerall, who was president at The Citadel when Willingham attended) appears as a distant authority, given to speechifying in outdated and stilted rhetoric. By the end of the novel, however, when we see him at close quarters, he is a more engaging figure: a man of great dedication and strength of will whose whole being is focused upon the daunting task of transforming 1600 cadets into officers capable of leading others into battle. His final speech to the cadets, on the occasion of de Paris' expulsion, is also the novel's last word on manhood. He reminds the assembly that the world is full of the shattered bodies and crushed spirits of men who have been unable to master themselves: "No youth can pass through four years of The Academy and not end as a man.... Think of that word; listen to it. *Man.* A simple monosyllable, but it has great force. Nothing is stronger than this word, for without the quality it signifies, the life of the race, and your own, is rendered utterly futile."

Of course, such a speech could not be delivered at The Citadel today, for among the assembly would be scattered a number of young women, whose presence at that venerable institution was mandated in 1995 by the 4th U.S. Circuit Court of Appeals in the name of equal opportunity.

Having read *End as a Man* with great interest, I paid a visit to The Citadel library to look up Willingham's picture in the 1941 number of the cadet yearbook, *The Sphinx*. Sure enough, there he was, smiling impishly, looking very much as he does on the dust jacket of the Vanguard Press first edition of the novel. What most drew my interest, however, were the faces of the 1941 graduating class, many of whom would soon see action in World War II. The maturity of those faces was striking; they were—most of them—the faces of men, so unlike the childish male visages that throng our campuses today in search of anything but self-mastery.

Zora Neale Hurston Beating a Tribal Drum.

ZORA NEALE HURSTON'S WHITE MARE

When novelist Zora Neale Hurston died penniless in a Florida nursing home in 1960, she was buried in a charity cemetery in an unmarked grave, an ironic resting place for a talented American writer and folklorist who, by all accounts, was a dazzling and memorable personality. Though her literary success (measured in sales numbers) had never been more than modest, the last twelve years of her life ushered in an almost complete eclipse of her fortunes.

The reasons for this are complicated. She had begun her career as a trained anthropologist (under the tutelage of Franz Boas) and folklorist whose first collection of southern black folktales, *Mules and Men* (1935), established her as a master of Afro-American dialect. Her best-known novels, *Jonah's Gourd Vine* (1934) and *Their Eyes Were Watching God* (1937), as well as her controversial autobiography, *Dust Tracks on a Road* (1942), drew heavily upon the folkloric idiom, one which she knew firsthand, having been born and raised in the all-black village of Eatonville, Florida. As long as her characters remained within a lower-class black milieu she was able to find willing publishers and avid readers. As Hurston explained in a 1950 essay, "What White Publishers Won't Print," black writers during the Jim Crow era were expected to conform to certain expectations. Either they confined themselves to the "unnatural history" of picturesque Negro stereotypes or they set themselves up as indignant protest novelists exploiting the "race problem," playing deftly upon liberal sympathies in the manner of Richard Wright. While Hurston's early novels were certainly not "unnatural" histories, they contained an element of the picturesque that appealed to white readers. However, when Hurston attempted to step outside the boundaries in her last published novel, *Seraph on the Suwanee* (1948), which was, in the words of her first biographer, Robert Hemenway, about "upwardly mobile white crackers," she was vilified, especially by the black literary establishment. Two subsequent novels, written in the 1950's, attempted to explore in realistic fashion the inner lives of affluent black characters. Both remained unpublished.

But the decline in Hurston's literary fortunes was also a result of her politics. Even during her earliest years as a rising star in the Harlem Renaissance, she had never been comfortable with the "black consciousness" advocacy of men like Alain Locke, W.E.B. DuBois, or the more radical Langston Hughes. Though Hurston benefited by her association with them, she considered the inner circle of the Harlem "Nigeratti," as she frequently called them, to be a rather effete cabal of well-to-do blacks who, despite their claims of "solidarity" with lower class blacks, had no real understanding of their lives. Hurston's break with the "Nigeratti" seems to have reached a critical point in 1942 when, in *Dust Tracks on the Road*, she penned a scathing indictment of the "race pride" movement that had its origins primarily in the political writings of DuBois. "Race Pride," she noted, "was something that, if we had it, we would feel ourselves superior to the whites. A black skin was the greatest honor that could be blessed [sic] on any man. A 'race man' was someone who always kept the glory and honor of his race before him." For Hurston, the concept of racial pride was flawed in two respects. It was, in the first place, a false abstraction. Endless talk of racial solidarity tended to obscure the rich profusion of differences within racial groupings, to subordinate the individual to the racial tribe. Even worse, racial consciousness promoted a collective resentment against whites that seemed to absolve blacks of any responsibility for their own condition. If blacks found themselves living in poverty, if black communities were rife with social problems, if black achievement was lagging far behind that of whites, then the fault could only lie with the white oppressor. The problem with such an argument is that it tends implicitly to cultivate a culture of inferiority. Individual failure can always be blamed upon external, racial factors.

While Hurston was by no means a friend of Jim Crow, a system she denounced on numerous occasions, she was wary of the exclusive focus on civil rights promoted by the "better- thinking negro," who ever more stridently called for political equality without providing poor blacks with the "tools" they needed to achieve real equality. Thus, she looked beyond the militancy of DuBois and the Harlem cabal (and their friends in the NAACP) to the example of Booker T. Washington, whose philosophy of self-help sought to empower individuals and local communities. She notes with barely concealed scorn how the "better-thinking negro" looked upon Washington "as absolutely vile for advocating industrial education" for blacks.

By contrast, left-leaning black leaders were already preparing the ground for the affirmative action policies of the present, policies which have worked to the advantage of the "better-thinking negro," while leaving the masses of poor blacks mired in a swamp of dependency. Indeed, Hurston was early on an adamant critic of the New Deal, precisely because it fostered a growing dependency, among both blacks and poor whites, on the Federal government. In her view, the New Deal was, no less than Reconstruction, an unwarranted expansion of government by executive decree. Never missing an opportunity to denounce FDR for both his domestic and foreign policies, she referred to him shortly after his death as "That dear, departed crippled-up-so-and-so [who] was the Anti-Christ long spoken of. I never dreamed that so much hate and negative forces could be unleashed on the world until I wintered and summered under his dictatorship." She characterized FDR's Depression-era relief program as "the biggest weapon ever placed in the hands of those who sought power and votes." As for the masses who accepted New Deal largesse, they "gradually relaxed their watchfulness and submitted to the will of the 'Little White Father'...."

For her candor Hurston was spurned by the liberal establishment and attacked by the likes of Langston Hughes, whose communist sympathies were well known, and who sought to portray Hurston as a traitor to the cause of black solidarity. But her greatest transgression against the dogma of racial pride was her denunciation of the Supreme Court's decision in *Brown v. Board of Education* (1954). The crux of Hurston's argument, published as a letter to the *Orlando Sentinel* in August, 1955, is that the stated intent of the Court—to ensure equality of education for black school children—was, in effect, a ruse. As is so often the case in her writing, she draws upon her store of Southern folk wisdom to present her case in quasi-allegorical fashion: "Those familiar with the habits of mules are aware that any mule, if not restrained, will automatically follow a white mare. Dishonest mule-traders made money out of this knowledge in the old days." One needed only to lead a white mare down a country road and "slyly open a gate, and the mules in the lot would ... follow this mare." In the *Brown* decision, a federally mandated end to segregation was the white mare used to lead black folk (the mules) into a new captivity, an illusory equality that promised little in the way of substantive improvement in the quality of black children's education.

Critics of Hurston's argument, then and now, often dismiss it with the claim that only a woeful ignorance of the poor quality of education in segregated black schools could explain her failure to support the Court's decision. But that isn't very likely. Hurston's own mother was a school teacher, Hurston herself worked, among her many jobs, as a substitute school teacher, and she travelled widely in the segregated South over the course of several decades.

What Hurston's critics have ignored—some self-styled "conservative" critics among them—are her apprehensions about the long-term implications of the *Brown* decision. Though she doesn't say as much in the *Sentinel* letter, it is likely that Hurston was fully aware that the *Brown* decision was reached, not upon Constitutional but psychological grounds. Among other studies cited by the Court was psychologist Kenneth Clark's finding that, when given a choice between black and white dolls, black children more often chose white dolls. From this Clark inferred from this that black children saw themselves as inferior, and the Court agreed. As one legal expert has recently asked, "Isn't it telling that the Court [did] not even attempt to explain the less-than-obvious connection between how a black child describes black and white dolls and the relative effect of integrated versus segregated schools on that child's 'feeling of inferiority'?" One might conclude, of course, as even some Constitutional originalists like Robert Bork have, that while the methodology of the *Brown* decision was flawed, the decision itself was nonetheless correct. If one measures correctness in this context by the achievement of a purely factitious equality, then perhaps Bork is right. But it is blindingly clear that, in the half century since the implementation of *Brown* began "with all deliberate speed," very little real improvement in the quality of public education for black children has been achieved. On the contrary the American public school system is scandalously dysfunctional, and, among other factors, *Brown* made this possible.

What Hurston understood better than most in 1955 was that the *Brown* decision was a flagrant attempt at social engineering by the Court, the sort of thing that has become all too frequent in recent decades. She warns in no uncertain terms against the implications of judicial activism: "In the ruling on segregation, the unsuspecting nation might have witnessed a trial balloon. A relatively safe one, since it is sectional and [concerns] a matter not likely to arouse other sections of the nation in support of the South. [But] ...a precedent has been established. Government by fiat can replace the Constitution." Hurston also understood that segregated black schools were important centers of cultural life in black communities all across the South, centers that provided cohesion and support for precisely the kind of "self-help" ethic that Booker T. Washington had worked tirelessly to cultivate. Indeed, Hurston's opposition to *Brown* was not at all eccentric, as many of her detractors claim. Many black teachers and administrators across the South shared her views. As Lynn Moylan notes, having surveyed a number of recent studies of the impact of *Brown*, "despite the lofty premises of *Brown*, ... the cultural connection and the vital sense of belonging and 'ethic of caring' characteristic of ... former all-black schools were in effect destroyed by the court system." Even former NAACP

Legal Fund attorney Derrick Bell, who at one time believed *Brown* to be the "Holy Grail of racial justice" has recently conceded that he was woefully mistaken, that in fact the Court should have enforced separate but equal funding for black schools.

Fifteen years after Hurston's burial in a pauper's cemetery, she was disinterred in the pages of *Ms. Magazine* when novelist Alice Walker published an essay there entitled "In Search of Zora Neale Hurston." In that essay Walker set the stage for the rebranding of Hurston's image, presenting the feisty, iconoclastic writer as a proto-feminist heroine and pioneering multiculturalist, while largely ignoring her politics. Today, Hurston's life has been made the subject of several biographies, most of her novels are in print, and she is studied widely in the academy. But it is a fair bet that most of the students exposed to Hurston's work rarely learn that she was a staunch conservative-libertarian thinker who would be appalled to discover that she has become an icon of the left-liberal establishment. It is true that in recent years some conservatives have attempted to reclaim her as one of their own. This is a perfectly legitimate endeavor, but one must be wary of easy generalizations. John McWhorter, in a recent piece in the *City Journal*, claims that Hurston was a "fervent Republican who would be at home today on Fox News...." This is doubtful, Yes, Hurston was a Republican, but she was as frequently critical of Republicans as she was of Democrats. Her closest political affiliations, especially in her last two decades, were with Old Right Republicans like Robert Taft, whom she openly supported during the Presidential campaign of 1951, and whose non-interventionist foreign policy was dear to her heart. Indeed, her denunciations of U.S. imperialism were frequent and bitter. In a passage expunged by the editors of the original 1942 edition of *Dust Tracks*, she wrote, "We, too, have our Marines in China. We, too, consider machine gun bullets good laxatives for heathens who get constipated with toxic ideas about a country of their own. If the patient dies of the treatment, it was not because the medicine was not good." One imagines that such remarks would not play well on Fox News.

The Crossroads Merchants

Standin' at the crossroad
I tried to flag a ride.
Didn't nobody seem to know me
Everybody pass me by.

I went to Charlotte in search of the New South and found it in a museum, the Levine Museum of the New South on 7th Street, in the Uptown district. Architecturally, the museum is a sheepish example of bland modernism, nothing to compare with its brash sister museums: the Bechtler Museum of Modern Art and the Mint Museum Uptown, veritable temples of postmodern irony. Like most historical museums, the Levine tells a familiar story: The New South is a narrative of "reinvention," and Charlotte epitomizes the New South *in toto*. Six hands-on "environments" illustrate the phases in Charlotte's long quest for distinction, beginning with the transformation of the Carolina Piedmont by the textiles industry in the 1880s. The War itself is mentioned merely as the catastrophic backdrop to this first defining moment of reinvention. The heroes in this narrative are not the defenders of southern sovereignty but those who rose up out of the defeat to adopt the sharp practices of the conqueror—the crossroads merchants and the builders of the mill towns which established Charlotte and the greater Piedmont as a dominant player in the empire of cotton.

Upon this foundation, we learn, Charlotte grew and prospered to become, first, a regional, then a national, and, finally, a transnational crossroads. Obstacles there were aplenty: rural poverty, ignorance, racism, nostalgia for the old ways of blood and soil, and religious intolerance. But the unbounded optimism of the Piedmont people happily overcame all of these, reinventing Charlotte anew with each passing generation, until she became, in the 21st century, a shining global city on a hill, her mills replaced by soaring glass towers, her rutted dirt roads by 10-lane expressways.

Of course, it would be boorish to expect a historical museum to present a *nuanced* account of the past. The casual visitor hardly expects to have his face rubbed in tragedy and ambiguity; he is seeking a smidgen of history, a little moral uplift, and a healthy dollop of entertainment—nothing more. He is reassured that Charlotte's miraculous ability to reinvent herself does not preclude a healthy respect for what is valuable about the past. Thus, contemporary Charlotte is upheld as a finely-tuned balance of political progress, savvy business sense and graceful southern tradition. Yet as I later ambled down Tryon Street on a sunny day in May, I saw little evidence of southern tradition. Indeed, every trace of the past, aside from a handful of memorial plaques, seems to have been erased.

In fact, erasure of the past has been the barely concealed theme of New South rhetoric (and practice) since its origins in the late 19th century. In an 1886 promotional speech, Henry Grady, the go-to godfather of the New South, implores his well-heeled northern audience to admire what the South has accomplished since 1865, to honor the valiant southern soldiers who, faced with the complete demolition of their economic system, built out of the bitter ashes a "brave and beautiful" city (Atlanta). Rest assured, he urges, Southerners of the rising generation are all about business, first and last: "We have learned that one northern immigrant is worth fifty foreigners, and have smoothed the path to southward, wiped out the place where Mason and Dixon's line used to be, and hung our latch-string out to you and yours." In short, the aim of the New South is to expunge any historical distinction between North and

South while reinventing the South in the image of the North. This is a bit like the Stockholm syndrome, is it not, in which captives begin to identify with their captors?

Tryon eventually brings me to State St. and Independence Square, the original Queen City crossroads. In every direction the banking towers thrust themselves skyward, hypermodern ziggurats where the strange gods of global capital are placated. All of them seem to have been built within the last 20 years, replacing an older, more modest generation of buildings whose neoclassical facades have vanished save for occasional "references" preserved at ground level. Independence Square is the most photographed location in the city. Each of the four corners features a monumental bronze sculpture: allegorical figures representing Industry, Transportation, Commerce and The Future. The latter depicts a female figure gazing at an upraised child, perhaps inspired by mythological goddesses of childbirth and destiny. The child himself is an image of the New South perpetually reborn and reimagined, and in truth the urban South these days is no longer so much a *place* as it is an idea of smiling, infantile futurity.

Less jejune is the representation of Commerce, which depicts a late 18th century gold prospector emptying his pan upon a head near his feet, said to be the head of Alan Greenspan, former director of the Federal Reserve. This may be apocryphal, but if not, the touch is a sly one, for the latest incarnation of Charlotte as a center of global finance owes much to the era of deregulation spawned by that New York banker and his cronies. Today, Charlotte is the nation's second largest banking center, and there is little doubt that financial giants such as Bank of America and Wells Fargo dominate not only the Uptown cityscape but, for the foreseeable future, virtually every aspect of the city's economic and political destiny.

How the banking industry achieved this position is a complex story, but origins are telling. After the collapse of southern banks in the aftermath of the War, thousands of poor yeoman farmers were unable to obtain credit. Unsupportable property taxes, foreclosures and falling crop prices forced many into tenancy or sharecropping, almost 93,000 by the turn of the century. The so-called "crossroads" merchants stepped into the breech, offering not only foodstuffs and agricultural supplies, but credit as well. Many of these merchant-creditors were local, but many were also northern opportunists. Passage of the notorious crop-lien laws gave the merchant bankers new powers to control how the farmers disposed of their yields; they were virtual monopolists in their realm, and interest rates were usurious—40% or higher in most cases. Given this level of indebtedness and the increasing reliance on cash crops (especially cotton), farmers were faced with higher levels of economic risk. Little wonder that many abandoned the land to seek greater security in the rising textile mill towns. But more of that in a moment.

I had arranged prior to my visit to Charlotte to join a local "meetup" group for a baseball matchup between the Charlotte Knights and the Durham Bulls at the BB&T (Branch Banking and Trust) stadium. My group consisted of roughly a dozen people, ranging in age from the early 20s to late 50s. We met at a watering hole not far from the stadium, then made a well-lubricated stroll to the ballpark. The Knights won that evening, but I can't say that I watched much of the game. We sat, or rather stood, in an area called the Home Run Porch, mobbed with chattering 20-somethings imbibing pricy craft beer. My companions proved to be a pleasant bunch, more than willing to speak to me about their experience of living and working in Charlotte. Most had lived in the city for a number of years; only one was a native. A number of them were employed in the banking industry or in one of the other Uptown corporate concerns. First impressions are often untrustworthy, but with one exception the group struck me as fairly typical of today's corporate "knowledge" class—affluent, secular, rootless, and well-versed in the urban arts of consumption. Most were drawn to Charlotte from northeastern cities by job opportunities, and stayed because they preferred the milder winters, the slower pace of life and the hospitality. Jillian and Daniel (not their real names), an older Jewish couple, were especially forthcoming on this subject. When I enquired whether they thought Charlotte was still a "southern" city, Daniel seemed dubious. I asked how often he met native Southerners. "Rarely," he said, "aside from the evangelicals I work with at the office." Detecting a hint of disapproval in his tone, I took the bait. "So, does southern religiosity bother you?" "It bothers me," he replied, "when they take it for granted that I need to be saved and invite me to church on Sunday. I'm Jewish!" Jillian agreed. I gathered it was a subject they had discussed between themselves before, and she implied that there was something insulting about evangelical proselytizing, though, she admitted, these approaches were generally polite. I didn't ask whether either of them ever attended their local synagogue.

Standing there in the Home Run Porch during the 7th inning stretch, gazing up past the field lights at the condominium towers of the city's Fourth Ward, thinking of the thousands of knowledge workers who must inhabit those towers, I reflected on the curious resemblance between this new more affluent proletariat and those who left their farms to live in the mill villages of the 1890s. Guiding lights such as D.A. Tompkins, who designed some of the earliest mill villages, were advocates of what historian Philip Wood has called "mill village paternalism." While Tompkins wrote glowingly of the benefits accruing to mill workers, it is clear that the villages were systems of social control intended to maximize profit. They were typically set apart from the "corrupting" influence of urban centers. Virtually all of the needs of the workers, or "operatives," as Tompkins called them, were provided for—housing, medical attention, village stores, schools, sanitation, leisure activities, and religious instruction. From the beginning, whole families rather than individuals were employed whenever possible, since married adults and their dependents were more pliable, and child labor, beginning at age 12, was cheap. Drawn to the villages out of dire need, the workers learned to accommodate radically new rhythms of work which transformed them into extensions of looms and spindles.

While there are some obvious differences, contemporary Charlotte, like many American cities, is not unlike a giant mill village. Charlotte is frequently upheld as a model of city planning, at least since the early 90s. Certainly, its compact Uptown approaches the New Urbanist ideal in some respects. Increasingly, the corporate towers are augmented by residential high-rises; in their shadow excellent restaurants, coffee shops, museums and galleries abound. Amusements are not in short supply. The nightlife is lively. The sports stadia and arenas are all within easy walking distance of many of the residential clusters. Moreover, Charlotte's impressive light rail system, still expanding, has created a number of smaller urban villages connected to the hub that enable residents to escape the traffic nightmares experienced by suburban dwellers.

Yet all this, too, is a system of social control, more subtle perhaps than the old mill villages, but all the more effective. Historians report that in the mill villages, workers were often well aware of the coercive nature of their captivity, and just as often found ways to resist—for example, by refusing to participate in village clubs or planned activities, or resisting with their bodies the production pace their overseers demanded of them. Today's corporate hirelings, by contrast, are hardly aware of the net that is drawn ever more tightly around them. They craft their makeshift identities out of consumer choices, or out of loyalty to corporate-sponsored teams like the Carolina Panthers, while clinging to a depthless political liberalism that is little more than a reflex affinity for what is approved and promoted by corporate media propagandists. When I asked my Meetup group about North Carolina's recent ban on any local "non-discrimination" ordinances that would allow individuals to patronize public bathrooms corresponding to their "gender preference" (a move which, in this case, was a direct response to an ordinance passed by the Charlotte City Council), the unvarying response was one of embarrassment mingled with a vaguely articulated assumption that "gender" is just one among other identity choices. Of course, in the new urban village that logic is impeccable, and accords well with the new regime: The ends of social control are best served by pandering to the illusion of self-fashioning, which seems to empower the self while drawing it more surely into slavery.

I drove out of Charlotte on the following morning with a powerful yen for Dixie, for that part of the South which the flood tide of globalization has, as yet, left high and dry—or, at least, where Battle Flags still fly defiantly over satellite dishes. Abandoning the interstate, I made my way through the piney woods of the Olde English country, out of the foothills and into the South Carolina midlands, past cotton fields and paper mills, over the Wateree and into the Santee basin where the Lowcountry begins. Here and across the rural Deep South, the New South never gained much traction, since it was and is an urban ideal. Of course, rural populations have dwindled substantially in recent decades, but millions still cling to their little patches of soil, often handed down over generations. The menfolk hunt and fish and barter for tools on Trade Day. Race isn't a big issue anymore. Just like their Caucasian counterparts, black men drive pickups and, often, listen to country music. The womenfolk marry early, raise babies and keep backyard gardens. Many of them shoot as well as their men, and learn at an early age the fine art of dressing deer and wild boar. On Sundays their churches are still full.

Until recently none of these folks were very political, but that may be changing. I saw Trump posters prominently displayed in convenience stores and bait shops. Ask these people what they think of Sen. Lindsay Graham and you might not get a polite answer. They have become increasing aware that the powers that be (in Washington, or in the state capitols, for that matter) are hostile powers. They may not be plotting revolution, but they are keeping their powder dry. Pleasant thoughts such as these buoyed my spirits as I made my way into Charleston, my home for some 20 years now. I have more than once been critical of the Holy City and the tourist industry that has been its life blood for decades. Nevertheless, after my sojourn in Charlotte I am more grateful than ever that here, in the once insurrectionist cradle of the Old South, the past is still a palpable presence. John C. Calhoun still broods on his 80-foot pedestal overlooking the street that bears his name. No one has as yet seriously suggested its erasure. Virtually everything in Charleston is a monument to something objectionable. To satisfy the vandals, the city itself would have to be erased and then rebuilt—a job for Charlotte's city planners, perhaps. [1]

---

[1] Sadly, since the final paragraph of this essay was composed several years ago, the Calhoun statue has, indeed, been erased. My account of that event can be found in *Chronicles of American Culture* (Dec. 2020).

The Original Carter Family, Founders of Country Music.

GOP Country

Somebody told me, when I came to Nashville
Son, you finally got it made
Old Hank made it here and we're all sure that you will.
But I don't think Hank done it this way

Back in February 2007, music historian J. Lester Feder's "When Country Went Right" appeared in *The American Prospect*. As Feder would have it, country music wasn't always as "conservative" as it is today. Once upon a time, it seems, country music was a left-leaning, "populist" American art form. Then Richard Nixon, taking his cue from George Wallace, invited country music stars to join him on the 1968 campaign trail. "Once fiercely allied with working people," claims Feder, country music married into the conservative movement and never looked back." It is certainly true that in recent decades mainstream country music has become increasingly identified with Republican politics, and that the music's fealty to its hillbilly and blue-collar origins has all too often been compromised by Nashville's craven appetite for popular acceptance (and the sales figures it generates). But the true story of country music's migration from the Democratic Dust Bowl to the Republican Tar Pit is a tad more complicated than what Feder chooses to reveal.

First of all, if I may follow Feder's lead and speak of country music as a populist art, then we will do well to remember that populism has always been Janus-faced. Since the golden days of William Jennings Bryan populist movements have generally championed the downtrodden factory worker, farmer, or middling small business owner against the interests of "elites," usually eastern bankers, railroad magnates, establishment politicians, or, more recently, pointy-headed intellectuals. Frequently, this defense of the "real producers" of wealth against the bloodsuckers who exploit them has taken the form of egalitarian political and economic positions. On the other hand, the "populist persuasion" (as Michael Kazin has called it) has generally been culturally and morally conservative, and especially so in the South. The most enduring motifs in country music have always been those of kinship and homestead, heartbreak and the hope of a better world in the hereafter. If country music has sometimes raised its blue-collar hackles in class-conscious anger or celebrated those it believed to be the political champions of ordinary folk, it has far more often been deeply apolitical, or, when political, atavistically so. This is perhaps due to the powerful strain of Calvinist religiosity so prevalent in the Appalachian Scots-Irish, whose balladry and fiddle playing have been the wellspring of country music since its commercial inception in the 1920s.

Nevertheless, during the Great Depression, when country music was still in its infancy (and when the distinction between "country" and "folk" music had not yet been firmly drawn), the populist impulse often found expression in lyrical laments for the poor farmer's plight in hillbilly songs with a political bent, such as Vernon Dalhart's "Farm Relief Song," first recorded in 1929, or Bob Miller's "Those Campaign Lyin', Sugar Coated Ballot-Coaxin' Low Down Farm Relief Blues." Some of Woody Guthrie's Dust Bowl ballads also possess an enduring populist pathos, though his best-known composition, "This Land is Your Land," vies with "We Are the World" for unadulterated banality. Yet Guthrie, who first achieved commercial success on country radio, borrowed the melody for that folk anthem from a gospel song, the Carter Family's "When the World's on Fire" (1930), and

I would argue that the finest country songs of the Depression era are those derived from the apolitical gospel tradition. Consider, for example, Alfred Brumley's haunting "I'll Fly Away" (1929), whose vision of liberation from a life of earthly toil has been taken up again and again by country and bluegrass singers: "When the shadows of this life have gone, I'll fly away; / Like a bird from prison bars has flown, I'll fly away (I'll fly away)."

If country music fans in the 1930s voted overwhelmingly Democratic, that is hardly surprising. After all, most of them were Southerners, and Southerners had *always* voted Democratic. But it is equally true that FDR was enormously popular in the South. In songs like W. Lee O'Daniel's "On to Victory, Mr. Roosevelt" or Billy Cox's "The Democratic Donkey is in His Stall Again," country singers celebrated FDR, scion of the eastern elite, as a populist hero. But the real story here is not about populist aspirations fulfilled in the warm embrace of an invalid who understood the heartbreak and misery of the landless and the unemployed. To be sure, FDR was a master of smooth and all-embracing populist rhetoric. At his first inaugural he proclaimed his salvific mission to cleanse the temple of American civilization of the predatory capitalists who had profaned it: "The money changers have fled from their high seats in the temple of our civilization. We may now restore that temple to its ancient truths ... social values more noble than mere monetary profit." But of course, as numerous critics of the New Deal have shown, FDR's true mission was not to drive out the money changers, but to invite them to sit down and break bread with the Pharisees of Labor, and to offer a desperate American people sanctuary in exchange for their self-reliance. This bargain with the Devil culminated in the proclamation of the Social Security Act, a secular vision of the Promised Land that seduced millions who should have known better.

During and after the Second World War, the popularity of country music began to reach well beyond the Sunbelt, spread by fiercely patriotic GI's and the millions of Southerners who migrated off the land and crossed the Mason-Dixon line in search of work. As this slow-motion diaspora unfolded, a subtle process of what has been called "southernization" occurred among the nation's working classes. As labor sociologist James N. Gregory has documented, by the early 1960's native born Southerners accounted for as much as 20% of the blue-collar labor force in key industrial sectors outside the South: auto and aircraft manufacturing, trucking, the steel and rubber industries, and the construction trades. To northern cities such as Detroit, Akron, Chicago, Baltimore and Columbus, or to western meccas like Los Angeles, San Diego, and Bakersfield southern laborers brought with them not only conservative cultural and moral values, but their religion, their love of stock car racing, and their music as well.

Bobby Bare's plaintive 1964 ballad "Detroit City" articulates the powerful nostalgia for the southern homes that these laborers abandoned:

'Cause you know I rode a freight train north to Detroit city,

And after all these years I find I've just been wasting my time.

So I think I'll take my foolish pride and put it on a southbound freight

And ride back to the loved ones,

The ones I left behind.

most of them never did return; they remained and spread their influence beyond the "Little Dixies" where they first congregated. Over time, country music became the musical voice, not just of the South, but of the American working classes, which in turn became increasingly conservative during this same period, years before the "right" turn that Feder describes.

This sociological and demographic development, though it is only one of several factors, is nonetheless a crucial one in understanding the eventual embrace of Republican politics by country music and its growing, increasingly middle-class, congregation of listeners. Equally important were changes in the agenda of the Democratic party and the dawning perception among significant numbers of the its traditional blue-collar constituency that the interests of the working man were no longer the party's first priority. Big Labor was increasingly seen as bloated and corrupt, its politics virtually indistinguishable from those of a federal bureaucracy committed to a radical Civil Rights agenda that seemed to threaten blue-collar job security as well as the integrity of working-class neighborhoods. Opposition to federally mandated bussing and massive welfare taxation were rampant among northern blue-collar Catholics, who needed no instruction from Southerners to recognize that their traditional way of life was imperiled. By 1968, with George McGovern's embrace of campus flag—not to mention feminist bra—burners, the Democratic abandonment of its traditional base was a *fait accompli*. Into this electoral breach stepped Governor Wallace, achieving significant northern victories in his 1964, 1968, and 1972 bids for the presidency, flanked by country music stars such as Tammy Wynette and Webb Pierce.

Country music was a bellwether of the changes transforming the American political and social landscape in the 1960s and early 1970s. When Merle Haggard recorded "Okie from Muskogee" and "The Fightin' Side of Me" (both in 1969), the response was overwhelming. What Nixon was calling the "silent majority" found its anthem in "Okie," for by then country music was no longer just hillbilly music; it had been discovered by millions of hard-working suburbanites—many of them just a generation removed from their blue-collar heritage—for whom the drug-induced excesses of rock music had no appeal. Appalled at the televised spectacle of the "free love" generation running amok on college campuses spewing anti-American hatred, they felt vindicated by Haggard's reactionary anger, just as their resentment of those who refused to work found an outlet in Guy Drake's 1970 hit "Welfare Cadillac." Rightly or wrongly, the swelling ranks of country music fans also supported the war in Vietnam, if only as a matter of national pride. Arguably, though, they were duped by the so-called "domino theory," just as their predecessors had been by the Social Security scam of the 1930s, and duped yet again by Nixon's adoption of the populist rhetoric of Wallace, shorn of its blue-collar bellicosity.

Certainly, it is the case that, after 1968, country music fans and evangelical Christians have been the core constituency of a Republican *faux* populism which, though it draws upon millions of blue-collar voters, is largely a middle-class phenomenon. To be sure, it is a cultural and moral, rather than an economic populism, and one combined with a traditional Republican emphasis on deregulation, the "free market," and reductions in Big Government. Under the Reagan and Bush administrations the federal government continued on an expansionist course, while the evangelical moral agenda amounted to little more than pious window dressing. Nonetheless, Nashville has been only too happy to supply the soundtrack to this supersized cozening of the American people. The list of Nashville luminaries who have performed at Republican election rallies, or provided endorsements and/or contributions to Republican candidates, is a long one, but includes (just to name a few) Toby Keith, Darryl Worley, Tanya Tucker, Sara Evans, Brooks & Dunn, Lee Ann Womack, Travis Tritt, Alabama, Loretta Lynn, Ricky Skaggs, Lee Greenwood, Reba McEntire, George Jones, George Strait, Hank Williams Jr. and Wynona Judd. For the reader who may not follow country music, every singer on this list is a top-drawer country act.

But endorsements are just the tip of the iceberg. Most of these stars have been promoted by a miniscule band of Nashville producers who are themselves, with a few notable exceptions, Republican stalwarts. Moreover, most of the more than 2,000 country music radio stations nationwide are owned by a few media conglomerates, including Cox Radio, Cumulus, and—the most powerful—Clear Channel, which also controls a huge share of the "conservative" talk radio format (Limbaugh, Beck, and Hannity among others) and is a well-known contributor of "soft money" to Republican campaign coffers. Clear Channel is widely believed to have conspired with Republican operatives to orchestrate the boycott of the Dixie Chicks after the March 2003 debacle in London, when radio stations from coast to coast refused to provide the Chicks airtime, reportedly because country music fans had "spontaneously" risen from their Barcaloungers by the tens of thousands to demand the silencing of little Natalie Maines (the Chicks lead singer), who had expressed her "shame" that the President of the United States was from Texas, her home state. Little conclusive evidence has emerged either to confirm or deny these persistent claims of behind-the-scenes shenanigans. Clear Channel executives, of course, claim that the uprising was indeed spontaneous, that its DJ's acted independently in response to hordes of angry fans, but it is doubtful whether Clear Channel DJ's have *ever* acted independently.

Over the course of many decades, populist sentiment has been shamelessly exploited by both wings of the American political duopoly, which require periodic infusions of populist blood to maintain their factitious vitality. What has changed in country music since the 1960s, however, is that Nashville's insatiable appetite for profit and respectability has driven a marketing agenda focused on capturing an ever-larger share of the middle-class consumer demographic. Thus, it has been willing to sacrifice its rural and blue-collar fan base in quest of a more lucrative suburban audience, one far more likely to drive SUVs than pick-up trucks. That this has coincided with GOP electoral strategy is, you might say, a happy coincidence for both.

Country music's transformation is perhaps best symbolized by the 1974 relocation of the Grand Ole Opry from the hallowed Ryman auditorium in downtown Nashville to a suburban site adjacent to a theme park, Opryland USA, just down the road from Andrew Jackson's Hermitage. (Appropriately enough, on opening night, Richard Nixon made an appearance and played a few piano tunes, just over a month before his resignation.) Before the theme park was shut down in 1997 and rebuilt as a shopping mall, country music fans and their families could take a cruise on the General Jackson Showboat or a wild ride on the Rock and Roller coaster, stuff themselves silly on corn dogs, then enjoy a show at the new Opry House. There they could listen to performances by traditionalist entertainers, chuckle over folksy Cracker Barrel radio commercials, and find themselves reassured by the illusion that country music was still, well, country. But in the 1990s the *real* action was unfolding in huge concert venues and stadiums across the country, where the likes of Garth Brooks and Shania Twain were strutting their stuff before adoring new metropolitan fans who hadn't the faintest idea that what they were listening to was about as country as MTV.

During the Bush *redux* era, the country music airwaves were dominated by youngsters who grew up listening to the Eagles and southern rock, and though they professed their admiration for Hank and George and Loretta, their music was often little more than pop music with a twang—the perfect soundscape for Republican election rallies. For the traditionalist who tuned his radio dial in hopes of hearing an oldie like Lefty Frizzell's "I Can't Get Over You to Save My Life," there was no satisfaction to be had. Instead, he found that the crying steel guitars of the past had all been buried beneath a sonic wall of synthesized, guitar-driven, neo-honky-tonk dreck. Of course, there were still some authentic country singers who somehow made the charts. George Strait continued to produce the same New Traditionalist country sound that he had pioneered in the 1980s, and Lee Ann Womack proved that honky-tonk angels still cheated (listen to her 1998 "I'd Rather Have What We Had" and get your hanky out). And then there was the young Gretchen Wilson, whose "Politically Uncorrect," an angry duet with Merle Haggard, was as country as it gets. But these were exceptions to the Republican rule in Nashville, where anything that might upset the soccer moms was generally *verboten.*

Nashville's low-rent rendezvous with the Republican party encountered some blowback in 2004, when a group of Nashville producers and performers formed an organization called the Music Row Democrats and supported the failed Kerry bid for the presidency. They were apparently under the impression that Kerry would, if elected, prove to be a more reliable advocate of the concerns of "ordinary Americans" than George Bush had proved to be. Indeed, there were and are Democrats in country music, a sizable number. Emmylou Harris, the queen of traditionalist singers, regularly campaigns for Democratic causes, as does Rodney Crowell, one of Nashville's best songwriters. Willie Nelson, long-time associate of Jimmy Carter, does his thing for the farmer, while the half-crazed Steve Earle badmouths Republican "fascists" at every opportunity. Even Toby Keith, whose "Courtesy of the Red, White, and Blue" (2002) promised to "put a boot" up the posterior of terrorist coddlers, claims to be a lifelong Democrat and praised Barack Obama in 2008, saying that he was the best Democratic candidate since Bill Clinton. Obama supporters in Nashville also included superstars Tim McGraw and Faith Hill, as well as Kelly Clarkson, who stated that she would vote for Obama over McCain because, although she was "not a hardcore feminist, we can't be going back to the 50s." Perhaps that inane remark had something to do with the presence of Sarah Palin on the Republican ticket, whom one pundit at *Salon* called a "Republican blow-up doll."

While it is no doubt the case that during the Trump years relatively few country music names have performed at MAGA rallies—in part because Mr. Trump seems to prefer rock singers like Ted Nugent—this doesn't mean that the long embrace between the country music fan base and the GOP has ended. On the contrary, that fan base, if charted demographically, would no doubt coincide closely with the map of red states in the 2016 and 2020 elections. It has been argued that Trump has moved the Republican party in a more authentically populist direction. That's debatable, of course. Certainly, he has brought out more blue-collar voters than his recent Republican predecessors, but we are seeing plenty of signs that GOP insiders are maneuvering to recapture the party. After all, the majority of Republican voters are suburbanites, especially in the South and Midwest, with little taste for actual populist revolt, and the country music fans among them are perfectly happy with the counterfeit currency minted in Nashville.

In short, the marriage between the GOP and country music isn't likely to end in D-I-V-O-R-C-E anytime soon. But surely the term "country music" (like the notion of a Republican populism) is by now all but a contradiction in terms. The sound produced in Nashville, the soundtrack for the lives of so many millions of Republican voters, is no longer rooted in the *country*—that is, in the agrarian America that gave it birth. This severance has been in the making for decades, and is virtually complete. I won't pretend to predict the future, but as I gaze toward that horizon, I don't see the likes of a Merle Haggard or a Johnny Cash reappearing. But any day now I expect "a boy named Sue" to emerge as the next big thing on Music Row. Oh, well, as the immortal Hank Williams once wrote, it's all just a "Jumbo lie an' a crow puss pie an' a Philly gunboat."

General William T. Sherman at Atlanta, Architect of the New South

BOOKS ARE FOR BLOCKHEADS!
OR, THE BUCKHEAD BOMBER

Recently, my old friend D.B. "Dukie" Kitchens phoned to inform me that I should soon expect in the mail an invitation to the inaugural Patriot Book Awards ceremony, to be held in Atlanta in late May. "What did I do to deserve this honor?" I asked. "Nothing," Dukie replied. "I got your name on the press list. It's an all-expenses-paid, booze-provided weekend, with gorgeous book-rep babes galore, and your old pal, *moi*, to guide you through the publishing underworld." I protested that I really had no interest in book awards, since nothing I cared to read had won an award for decades. Besides, I said, "Atlanta makes me break out in existential hives."

But Dukie was insistent. This is not your ordinary book award, he said. "This is a *conservative* books award." "Conservative!" I chortled. "What does that mean? Are the nominations certified by some Tea Party focus group?" "Not quite," said he, "but if you'd occasionally pull your Luddite nose out of the 19th century, you'd know all about this. Fox News has been pumping it up for weeks. The offer began to sound tempting. I hadn't been out of the Lowcountry for a coon's age; a bourbon-drenched weekend in a posh hotel might be just the thing.

Several weeks later, as I motored out of Charleston on a Friday morning I reflected on what I had learned about the Patriot Awards. A conservative response to the liberal dominance of the American literary scene and its signature prizes—the Pulitzer, the National Book Award, et al.—the Patriot prize was being touted by conservative pundits as more genuinely representative of the wholesome common sense and good taste of the American people—not just a cabal of New York publishers, writers, literary critics and *soi-disant* guardians of high culture. As a move in the public relations game, this was savvy enough. After all, the populist appeal to American "common sense" has a long history, and any suggestion that the literary "taste" of the average American might be mediocre at best is bound to invite indignant charges of elitism. According to the Patriot Awards website, the prizes in five categories (fiction, poetry, autobiography, biography, and non-fiction) would be awarded democratically. The usual panel of literary "experts" would be eschewed. Publishers would nominate one book in each category and those books would be sent to representative groups of readers. The Awards' sponsor, the somewhat sinister-sounding Committee for the (Re)Occupation of Middle America (COMA), would select readers from every class, ethnicity, and sexual orientation, as well as from a broad variety of occupational and educational backgrounds. To ensure that everything remained objective, a third-party, the NSA, would oversee the process, maintain secrecy, and tabulate the results after readers ranked the nominated titles.

As I entered the ever-mushrooming outskirts of Atlanta, I puzzled over why this flashy icon of the New South might have been chosen as the locale for the Patriot Awards. If Nashville is the Buckle on the Bible Belt, then Atlanta might aptly be called the Rhinestone in its Bellybutton, assuming, of course, that the belly is hanging well below the buckle. But perhaps I am being unfair. Maybe we were to imagine the Patriot Awards as a symbolic rising out of the ashes, the beginning of a renaissance in American letters? Improbable, yes, but who knows? I resolved to stifle my cynicism—with a little help from Jack Daniels.

That resolve was soon rewarded as I checked into my room at the Marriott Buckhead, where the ceremony was to be held, and found it well stocked. Half past three was a bit early to imbibe, but, what the hell, I thought, and, as I gazed out my window upon the high-tech sprawl of Hotlanta, I lifted my shot glass in a silent toast to General Sherman, who made it all possible. But my reveries were soon interrupted by an annoying buzz in my pocket—a text message from Dukie: "In the lounge. Let's shake and bake, Mr. Pibb." Dukie and I go way back, so far back that I can't even remember when or why he first began calling me Mr. Pibb. We spent many a summer evening mullet fishing in the backwaters of Mobile Bay and roomed together as undergrads. He's one of the best investigative journalists in the country and, despite his many faults, a loyal friend. I threw on a blazer and made for the lounge.

I should have known that Dukie wouldn't be alone. He was seated at the bar wearing the same old gap-toothed grin, and next to him perched a raven-haired young thing who might have passed for 21. Her name was Kaylie, which didn't quite match her look: black boots, black jeans, and a tight black t-shirt, upon which was embossed the face of Ayn Rand in a style curiously resembling those ubiquitous images of Che Guevara in his iconic jaunty red beret. "Pleased to meet you," I said, seating myself atop a plush barstool, while a shot of Jack appeared mysteriously in front of me. Kaylie offered a smile that might just as well have been a sneer. Maybe it was the three piercings in her lower lip and the one in her right nostril that gave me that impression.

"Kaylie's a journalism major at Emory," Dukie informed me with a wink. "She's from Savannah." Dukie had been living in Atlanta for several years, and occasionally taught classes in the evenings to make ends meet, so I took the wink to mean that Kaylie was a student of his. In any event it was clear that she resented my intrusion and responded to my inquiries about her career plans in clipped monosyllables. Dukie seemed to find her rudeness enormously amusing. As the lounge began to fill with Happy Hour tipplers, most of them conspicuously over-coiffed, I was reminded of a Republican campaign rally I'd written up last year.

Hoping to direct Dukie's attention to the job at hand, I asked: "Are most of these people here for the awards?" Gazing into the mirror behind the bar he replied. "Oh, yes. That's Megyn Kelly, the Fox News anchor, over there at the window table." Turning, I saw a tallish blonde surrounded by a gaggle of baby-faced male twenty-somethings. "Does she know anything about books?" I asked. Dukie rolled his eyes. "She was a corporate litigator before she became a news babe. Those people don't read books. Just teleprompters. But she's eye candy, Mr. Pibb, and she pulls an audience—a very big audience." I wondered aloud whether Kelly was to be the MC at the main event on Saturday evening. "Oh, *no*," Dukie intoned. "The COMA wanted a little more, shall we say, *gravitas* for their money. Pat Sajak got the nod."

As we moved from the lounge to the Marriott dining room I mulled over the significance of using a popular game show host as the MC at a literary event. Dukie explained what I should have known—that Sajak had been an advocate of conservative causes for years, sat on the Board of Trustees for Hillsdale College, and, most importantly, was one of the Directors of Eagle Publishing. Eagle, of course, is the parent company of Regnery / Gateway, as well as the publisher of *Human Events* and *RedState.com*, not to mention owner of the Conservative Book Club.

As we made short work of our *filet mignon*, Dukie surveyed the dining room. "Perhaps you haven't noticed Mary Matalin over there, former campaign director for Dubya, now Executive Editor at Threshold Editions, publisher of Dick Cheney's *In My Time*." Threshold, I learned, is the conservative Simon and Schuster imprint. "Or cast your eyes in the other direction, Mr. Pibb. See the lady in red? That's Dana Perino, former Bush White House press secretary, sometime Fox News commentator, now Executive Editor at Crown Forum, the conservative imprint at Random House." "It all seems," I commented, "a bit incestuous."

Dukie's point wasn't really about politics, but profits. Book awards, he insisted, had always been about selling books, not about promoting good literature. The National Book Award, for instance, was established in 1936 by the American Booksellers Association. The Patriot Awards were heavily backed by conservative booksellers and had close ties to conservative news media, and all these people are adept at targeting their market. In this case the market is an estimated 50 million plus potential readers whose politics tend to be socially conservative. Crown Forum may be the embarrassing stepchild in the Crown Publishing family, but Random House executives chuckle all the way to the bank.

After Dukie promised to meet me for breakfast the next morning, I returned unsteadily to my room and contemplated the state of American literature in 2013. Very few American publishers of any size are now independent; most are owned by conglomerates, and few are prepared to take risks on books that don't promise to sell hundreds of thousands of copies on the first print run. Novelists, for example, who aspire to write for serious adult readers are out of luck. Consider *USA Today's* top one-hundred sellers of the last 20 years. Seven out of the top ten are all titles by J. K. Rowling. Stephanie Meyer and Dan Brown. To find a novel that might be worthy of being read generations hence, you must scan down to number 22, *To Kill a Mockingbird*, written over 50 years ago. Aside from reprints like *Mockingbird* and *Catcher in the Rye*, there is nothing in the top 100 that anyone in the year 2525 will care to read, assuming that by then literate Americans have not been placed on the endangered species list.

Ironically, as the number of Americans who might be thought serious readers continues to diminish, the number of literary prizes on offer has risen absurdly. Wikipedia lists 223 of them in the U.S. Have you heard of the Lulu Blooker Prize? That's for "books based on blogs." How about the Native Writers Circle of the Americas awards? In short, one need not be unduly cynical to assume that the indecent proliferation of prizes is an index of the publishers' desperate desire to find or create new markets for their wares.

I found Dukie alone in the dining room on Saturday morning, nursing his second Bloody Mary. "Where's your punkette?" I asked. "Who knows," growled Dukie. "She'll turn up this evening, I'm sure." I thought to inquire: "What are her politics? I couldn't help but notice the Ayn Rand t-shirt." Dukie grunted. "She calls herself an "anarcho-libertarian-paleo feminist." He sat in silence for a bit, then abruptly seemed to recall our conversation of the evening before: "All of these award ceremonies are 'pseudo-events' anymore. Everything is calculated for media impact. The only thing that matters is that the ceremonies get noticed. *Any* publicity is good publicity. Scandal is best of all." "Is something scandalous likely to happen at tonight's ceremony?" I wondered. "You never know," Dukie said, somewhat ominously. "Let's stroll over to the exhibition area and check out the book-rep babes."

The exhibition was held in one of the Marriott's smaller ballrooms, where dozens of tables had been set up by publishers that had either nominated books for the awards or were simply displaying their recent titles. The place was crawling with book buyers for the big chains. Frankly, it was hard to pay much attention to the books when the reps were so much more attractively packaged. "Damn," I said, "I've seen one or two sexy book reps in my day, but these girls look more like a cheerleading squad." Dukie smiled. "You hit the nail on the head, Mr. Pibb. These girls are all Falcons cheerleaders, but don't ask 'cause they won't tell." I was nonplussed. "You mean the COMA hired these girls just for the event?" "Exactly," said Dukie. "They've probably all memorized a little spiel to promote the books." With all that cleavage on display, I thought, they really didn't need to say anything at all.

Dukie and I happily walked through the aisles of booths, ogling the titles. Sue Monk Kidd's *Dancing with Mystical Bees* seemed to be attracting a nice crowd. Steven King's autobiography, *My Life as a Literary Shock Jock*, was attracting notice, especially since an Amazonian blonde in blood-red stilettos was handing out review copies to the press. Over at the Little-Brown booth, stacks of Malcolm Gladwell's *The Sacred Chao* were prominently displayed, but the most interesting were, naturally, the political selections. Virtually all of them bore conservative imprints. At the Crown Forum table,

BOOKS ARE FOR BLOCKHEADS! OR, THE BUCKHEAD BOMBER

Charles Krauthammer's *How the War on Terror Builds American Character* was the center of a small frenzy. Just across the aisle, at Threshold Editions, Marco Rubio's *Brown Like Me* was being touted as the sequel to his recent memoir, *An American Son*. "Is this a joke?" I asked Dukie. "Not at all," he replied. "The Senator argues that legal immigration from Latin American, especially female immigration, should be tripled. He claims that not only do Hispanics grow more businesses, but their women are more fertile." He paused. Then added with a wink: "The idea is that massive intermarriage between conservative Caucasian men and Hispanic women is the only thing that will save the Republican Party."

Eventually, Dukie dragged me away from the exhibition hall and back to the lounge. By the time the evening's main event rolled around, both of us were cross-eyed. The ceremony, scheduled to start at six, was a black-tie event, and I somehow managed to squeeze into my old tux and make my way to the Grand Ballroom. Luckily, I found our name cards on a table well to the rear and out of the way. A shifty-looking waiter of indeterminate sex had just arrived with a carafe of white wine when Dukie and Kaylie made their entrance.

I was astonished at the transformation. Kaylie, sans piercings, had remade herself in the spitting image of Audrey Hepburn in *Breakfast at Tiffany's*: black evening gown, black velvet gloves up to the elbows, her hair arranged in an elegant *chignon*—everything but the long cigarette holder. Speechless, I looked at Dukie, who just shrugged. Looking more than a bit ragged around the edges, he wasn't likely to last through the ceremony. With each new course, he grew more comatose while Kaylie and I carried on a charming conversation, if you can imagine Audrey Hepburn as an anarcho-libertarian-paleo feminist.

As for the ceremony, it was, at the outset at least, hopelessly dull. Pat Sajak seemed lost without Vanna. The winners in the various categories were all very well behaved and quite predictable. You've heard all about them by now, of course. Lindsay Graham's tearjerker, *A Bachelor for Life,* was widely expected to win best autobiography, and did—by a landslide. Not even the Poetry prize for Maya Angelou's *Twenty-One Ways of Eating Jim Crow* was really unexpected, particularly since it was an Oprah's Book Club selection. My readers do not, of course, need to be reminded that the nonfiction award went to David Horowitz for his *Paleoconned: Treason on the Right*. Horowitz received tremendous applause for an acceptance speech that vociferously denounced the deviousness of the paleo fifth column, which disguises its collaboration with America's enemies under the cover of "traditional values."

Media reports have been somewhat confused about what happened next, but I recall distinctly that just as Sajak was about to announce the fiction award, the lights were suddenly extinguished and several small explosions erupted in the area around the stage. Smoke filled the room and pandemonium broke out. Someone yelled "Stink bombs!" And, indeed, my nose began to fill with the nauseating odor of rotting flesh. I looked around for Dukie and Kaylie, but they had disappeared! Making for the door I was all but stampeded by the frightened crowd, while alarms began to wail. Piercing the din a shrill woman's voice could be heard shouting over and over, "Squeal you Republican Pigs! You pseudo-capitalist running dogs! Books are for blockheads!" And I could swear that, as I took a last look back at the stage, the diminutive figure holding the microphone was shaking a black velvet fist!

The Flamingo Kid

It is a truism to note that H. L. Mencken, like his great vitriolic predecessor, Jonathan Swift, was a thoroughgoing misanthrope. So jaundiced was Mencken's vision of human existence that he preferred to read *King Lear* as farce rather than tragedy—since nothing, he was fond of saying, could be more farcical than death. But if Mencken's loathing for his fellow man prevented him from discovering some remnant of dignity in the antics of the intelligent ape, it made him one of our most acute observers of the American political scene. "Mirth," Mencken wrote in his "On Being an American," "is necessary to wisdom.... Well, here is the land of mirth, as Germany is the land of metaphysics and France is the land of fornication. Here the buffoonery never stops."

The American "buffoonery" that so regaled Mencken was of the unconscious sort, the buffoonery of those, especially in political life, whose grotesquely inflated sense of their own self-importance provides the rest of us with endless mirth. Yet Mencken's own satiric art was itself a kind of buffoonery, albeit of the wickedly honed and self-conscious variety, and one intended to remind us that the moment we begin to take American politics *too* seriously we join the parade of unconscious buffoons. Thus, Mencken would approve, I suspect, of Rep. John Graham Altman, III (R.- Charleston District

119), a politician who, for several decades of public life in South Carolina, supped among the scribes and Pharisees with tongue planted firmly in cheek.

Everyone in these parts remembers the "dress code" incident at the State House in Columbia, when, during the 2001 legislative session, an overzealous clerk's office in the House forbade female pages to wear blouses exposing cleavage or skirts more than four inches above the knees. Shortly thereafter, a memo was released by a group calling itself the "Men's Caucus," instructing the pages to ignore the dress code. Instead, "they should save valuable materials used in blouse construction" and consider undergarments strictly "optional." They were further encouraged to regard "the terms 'babe,' 'honey,' 'sugar,' and 'little missy' as compliments and terms of endearment." Although authorship of the Men's Caucus memo remains a well-guarded secret, it is widely rumored that Rep. Altman was one of the "handful of Republicans" responsible. Of course, virtually all the Democrats in the House waxed apoplectic over the incident, obliging state Attorney General Charlie Condon to call for a State Law Enforcement Division (SLED) investigation of the matter. Well, that was a bit like using a pile-driver to kill a fire ant. The unsurprising upshot was that, six months later, the General Assembly was compelled to hold a sexual harassment seminar for its members. When asked whether he would be attending the seminar, Rep. Altman was widely reported as saying, "I won't be able to come. I forgot to pack a dress."

Altman got his start in local politics back in 1976 when he was elected to the Charleston County School Board, subsequently serving in that capacity for twenty years. Then, as now, the progressive worthies on the board regarded him as their *bête noire*, and no doubt with good reason. Altman obstructed or attempted to obstruct every politically correct piece of nonsense proposed by the board during those years. Perhaps most memorable was his proposal—a *riposte* to those calling for an official Black History month—that Charleston County schools observe a White History month every March. Of course, the proposal never got off the ground, and Altman himself later admitted that he did it "just to make a point. I told the other board members not to be stupid and vote for it" (as if there was ever any danger of that!). Nonetheless, Altman was predictably branded a racist and white supremacist (dirt clods that continue wrongfully to be flung at him at every opportunity). After twenty frustrating years of bickering with the educrats, Altman retired from the school board. Later, he vented some of that frustration: "There are more people in Charleston County that believe in the tooth fairy," he lamented, "than people who believe in the school board."

But to his credit, Rep. Altman has continued to work tirelessly for local control of schools, for real parental involvement in decision-making, and, most recently, for returning authority to teachers in the classroom. Ironically, these very efforts have drawn Altman into a running battle with the organization that, traditionally, might have been most supportive. When early in 2005 Altman signed on as a backer of Governor Mark Sanford's "Put Parents in Charge" initiative, he was opposed by the hired muscle of the national PTA.

In an editorial published in a number of papers across the state, Altman accurately depicted today's PTA as little more than a PAC: "What happened to the old PTA?" he wondered. "One year [when] I was on the school board, I joined 32 PTAs and went to a meeting every week. Now the PTA is just the political arm of whatever educrat blob there is out there." Needless to say, that didn't go over well with the PTA's local defenders. *Charleston City Paper* pundit, Bill Davis, responded in his usual patronizing fashion: "Poor John Graham Altman just can't seem to get his mind around the concept that the PTA has shrugged off its apron and put down its sheet of cookies to knot its neck scarf and pick up a briefcase." A briefcase, indeed. Many who lived in Altman's district were just grateful that there were some ideas that poor John Graham just couldn't get his mind around.

Even his most persistent detractors admit that Rep. Altman's traditionalist advocacy for state and local sovereignty is genuine. In the late 1990s, for example, Altman was among the most vocal opponents of the video poker gambling industry, a corrupt enterprise that had managed by a piece of stealth legislation to gain a sleazy toehold in the state back in 1989. Known in the industry as "convenience gambling," video poker in South Carolina was firmly established by 1997 and raking in profits estimated at 2.8 billion, only a small percentage of which ever made its way into state coffers. While most opponents railed against the demoralizing effects of video gambling, Altman remained focused on the big picture. "Money talks, money talks," he said. "South Carolina is no longer a sovereign territory. We are occupied by the forces of organized gambling."

More recently, in April 2005, after the South Carolina Supreme Court struck down a Charleston County ordinance that would have placed caps on property assessment increases for tax purposes, Rep. Altman introduced a constitutional amendment intended to allow counties to secede from the state—at least for the purpose of tax valuation. "Property tax is a monster that is devouring our Charleston community, " Altman told the *Post and Courier*. "We pass bill after bill to try and get property tax relief.... I was thinking of how to get us around the constitution. So, I decided to take us out of the constitution." While local progressives argue that the property tax cap was intended to protect the rich, Altman in fact spoke for the overwhelmingly middle-class majority in his district, whose tax assessments in one of the hottest real estate markets in the country are eating away at their children's college funds.

While the South Carolina chapter of the League of the South has consistently awarded Rep. Altman its "Patriot" designation for his legislative performance, others—blacks, liberal women, and homosexuals—would be only too happy to see him hogtied and castrated (that is, if their cuddly views of human nature allowed them to admit to such vengeful fantasies). Indeed, sometimes Altman seems to relish baiting such victim groups with an almost Mephistophelian glee. In March of 2000, he joined a number of State House Republicans in opposing a proposed Martin Luther King holiday, a measure which would make South Carolina the last state in the nation to so honor the civil rights leader. Altman, at a crucial moment in the debate, took the floor and began to quote from a biography of Dr. King which, according to the *South Carolina News*, "alleged that the civil rights leader had extramarital affairs and plagiarized parts of his college papers." Altman's point was that, while it would be appropriate to celebrate a "Civil Rights

Day," King himself was unworthy of such an honor. "You can run from the real Martin Luther King," he said, "but you can't hide from him!" Enter the chorus of breast-beating accusers, led by House Minority Leader, Gilda Cobb-Hunter, maligning Altman as one of those white supremacist bigots of yesteryear who slandered the spotless civil rights leader out of sheer hatred for his cause. No one, not even the "conservative" *Post and Courier*, bothered to name the biography in question or to report honestly that the charges against King have long since been established beyond any reasonable doubt.

A few months later, during the acrimonious debate over whether the Confederate flag should be removed from the State House dome, Altman further infuriated the black and liberal communities when he said, "We must say to those folks who feel crippled, rightly or wrongly, by this [flag issue]: Quit looking at symbols, get out and get a job, quit shooting each other, quit having illegitimate babies." During the same debate, Altman wrote a letter to Education Secretary Barbara Nielsen after she came out in support of removing the flag: "The kindest help I can offer you," he wrote to Nielsen, "is to get you quickly qualified for the Federal Witness Protection Program." In response to claims that his letter could be considered a threat, Altman countered, "I'm not a threat to her. She's a threat to our children." When Altman learned that, to appease the NAACP, The Citadel had resolved to remove its own Confederate flag from public view, he managed to kill two lovebirds with one stone: "I never thought," Altman told the press, "that we'd find The Citadel Board of Visitors and the NAACP holding hands and whispering sweet nothings."

The *Post and Courier* once characterized Rep. Altman as a "quote machine," but it is not only the lash of his tongue that enrages his sanctimonious opponents—it's also his taste in lawn décor. Next time you are in Charleston, take a drive down Folly Road toward the southern end of Altman's district and you will see what I mean. Just across from the Earth Fare supermarket, our local whole foods mecca where the vegans and the New Age *cognoscenti* gather for worship on Sunday mornings, you will find the Altman house, where John Graham resides with his lovely wife, Charm. I say "resides," but in fact the place—a sort of ramshackle mini-mansion with peeling columns and a fake balcony plastered above the front door, situated at one of the busier intersections in Charleston—has a desultory air of desertion about it. The plastic pink flamingos on the lawn are the only evidence that the Altmans actually *inhabit* the house. From time to time, John Graham and Charm enjoy dressing up the flamingos in cute little costumes. Reportedly, the birds were on one occasion decked out in nuptial attire. But what really riled the Earth Fare crowd was the time the Altmans painted half the flamingos black and made pointy white hats for the other half. Or so it has been rumored; I didn't personally witness the affront. One local blogger claims to have it on good authority that the event did occur. "Apparently," he writes, [the Altmans] feel that there is nothing more festive than a mock lynching." What is truly laughable is that anyone would take such buffoonery so seriously. The costumed flamingos are really just "good ole boy" political theater. Install those same bedizened flamingos in one of our *chi-chi* art spaces downtown, and you'd have the art mavens praising them as bold and provocative postmodern agitprop.

Rep. Altman was involved in another piece of political theater in 2005 that brought him briefly into the national limelight, though the occasion was not of his own making. The furor erupted in April after the House Judiciary Committee considered bills intended to make both cockfighting and domestic violence felonious offenses. The Judiciary Committee passed the "gamecock" bill but tabled the domestic violence bill—both in the same week. Rep. Gilda Cobb-Hunter, a sponsor of the latter bill, naturally seized upon the opportunity afforded by this spectacular case of bad timing: "What we have said by the actions of the Judiciary Committee is we aren't going to create a felony if you beat your wife [or] partner. But now, if you've got some cockfighting going on, whoa! Wait a minute." Within hours, it seemed, a Sherman's army of women's advocacy groups had stormed into Columbia to protest. When reporter Karen Gormley of Columbia's Channel 10 (WIS-TV) News and her camera crew cornered Altman (a Judiciary Committee member) in his State House office, Gormley confronted him with the invidious comparison between cockfighting and domestic violence suggested by Cobb-Hunter. Altman's reply and the subsequent "dialog" are savory enough to quote in full:

Altman: "People who compare the two are not very smart and if you don't understand the difference, Ms. Gormley, between trying to ban the savage practice of watching chickens trying to kill each other and protecting people's rights in [criminal domestic violence] statutes, I'll never be able to explain it to you in a 100 years, ma,am."

Gormley: "That's fine if you feel you will never be able to explain it to me, but my question to you is: Does it show that we are valuing a gamecock's life over a woman's life?"

Altman: "You're really not very bright and I realize you are not accustomed to this, but I'm accustomed to reporters having a better sense of the depth of things.... To ask the question is to demonstrate an enormous amount of ignorance. I'm not trying to be rude or hostile, I'm telling you."

Gormley: "It's rude when you tell someone they [sic] are not very bright."

Altman: "You're not very bright and you'll just have to live with that."

Later in the interview, when Gormley pointed out that South Carolina's current domestic violence law regards such violence as a misdemeanor even on the second offense, Altman (himself an attorney who has defended battered women) replied, "There ought not to be a second offense. The woman ought not to be around the man. I mean you women want it one way and not another. Women want to punish the men, and I do not understand why women continue to go back around the men who abuse them."

Rep. Altman's "insensitivity" towards the women who "go back around the men who beat them" was, by the following day, splashed all over the cable networks and the *New York Times*. The infallibly sensitive *Miami Herald* columnist, William Pitts, saw the incident as proof that "plucky little South Carolina" had "shot to the head of the pack" in the competition for "Most Backward State in the Union." Of course, given the state of the Union, that's a pretty flattering distinction. Still, it must be admitted that Altman could have spoken, shall we say, more ... *feelingly* on the subject of domestic violence.

There are perfectly sound reasons to question the need for special laws for domestic violence (or "hate crimes," or "gay rights"). Unfortunately, councilor Altman (who should, and probably does, know better) failed to articulate those reasons. In the first place, domestic violence laws rarely consider the frequency of cases in which the battered woman *initiates* the violent encounter with her spouse (or "partner"). Recently, even some feminists have begun to admit that "one size fits all" domestic violence laws fail to consider the complexity of the relationships involved. Most ominously, many such laws require that once an incident of domestic violence (no matter how trivial) has been reported, an arrest *must* be made. As Linda Mills, feminist and author of a recent controversial book on the subject has noted, "To take crucial decisions about prosecuting a case out of these women's hands serves only to disempower them and to deny their personal agency." Her jargon notwithstanding, Ms. Mills has a point, though a conservative might argue that the removal of such "crucial decisions" from the woman is not so much an attack upon her "personal agency" as it is a subversion of the marriage bond (at least in those cases where the partners are, in fact, husband and wife).

In any event, in the wake of the Gormley affair and the public outcry that followed, Rep. Altman came within a hair's breadth of being censured by the House. To the disappointment of many, he capitulated under enormous pressure and delivered a public apology for his remarks. Now whether that apology was altogether sincere is a different matter. To my ears it sounded more like vintage Altman buffoonery. Speaking before a packed State House, he said, "I'm sorry I caused pain to those to whom I really caused pain, and I'm sorry I caused pain to anyone who might want to say 'ouch' anyway." Then he made curious reference to "some people I offended that I didn't offend ...," and lamented the "feeding frenzy" in the media that threatened freedom of speech. "I don't mind dining out now and then," he added, "but I don't always like being the entrée. It's been roast pig for the last week." While the

Republican leaders in the state House and Senate, along with the editorial board of the *Post and Courier*, pretended to believe the apology sincere, Gilda Cobb-Hunter called his bluff: "[Altman's] been allowed to get away with this buffoonish behavior for years.... This is nothing but partisan damage control."

When Altman announced early in 2006 that he would not be running for reelection, he made good on his claim that "the best politics is no politics." To be sure, the neocon Republican establishment (not to mention the Democrats) were thrilled to be rid of a colleague they considered an embarrassing reminder of the bad old days when a man who battered his wife was too busy hiding from her kinfolk to worry about the law. Nonetheless, his departure was a great loss for Charleston. Rep. Altman has served her interests loyally and wittily for decades. Some would disagree about the "wit," of course, but judge for yourselves: Shortly after the Massachusetts Supreme Court legalized "gay marriage," Altman was the man who coined the phrase "black robe disease" to describe the contagion afflicting judges who compulsively legislate from the bench—and that is surely a nomenclature worthy of adoption by the Centers for Disease Control over in Atlanta.[1]

---

[1] John Graham Altman, III, passed away in November, 2013—on Election Day, appropriately.

Sheet Music Cover for "I Wish I was in Dixie," 1900

DIXIE FOR DUMMIES

Many readers are probably already familiar with Regnery Publishing's Politically Incorrect Guide series, two of which have achieved bestseller status in recent years. One of the books in the series, Clint Johnson's *Politically Incorrect Guide to the South (and Why it Will Rise Again)* provokes me to ponder the difference between bonafide southern pride, on the one hand, and its *faux* wannabe cousin, on the other. Johnson claims to be from a small town in Florida, called Fish Branch, and currently lives in North Carolina. I say "claims to be" because I suspect that Johnson is really a Connecticut Yankee who, having moved to the South in the recent past, has had a "born again" experience. I have looked at a map of Florida, and no such place as Fish Branch appears there. Admittedly, it may be a very small town, so small that it doesn't rate a dot on a map. But I wonder whether Fish Branch may in fact be a figment of Johnson's imagination. Perhaps he is so deeply abashed by his northern origins that he has repressed the hateful memory.

Why should I make such a libelous assertion? Well, perhaps it is that, like so many religious converts, Johnson defends his new faith with all the fervor of a crusader. So, one might object, what is wrong with that? Southerners have always fervently defended their beloved homeland. That's quite true. But if Johnson is really a Southerner, his mama and daddy must have neglected to teach him that boasting is bad manners. But to say as much would be to slander Johnson's parents. No, Johnson can't be a Southerner, simply because Southerners *never* boast.

According to Johnson, the South is patently superior to the North (or any other region of the country) in every respect worth mentioning. Southern folkways are the most distinctive, and southern speech the most poetic. Southern cuisine is the most delectable, while southern women are the most ... well, *delectable*. While Southerners are musical and make the only American music worth listening to, Northerners are tone deaf. Southerners still cling loyally to the old-time religion, while Northerners (and otherners) worship liberal idols and the almighty dollar. Southerners don't care so much about money, yet, paradoxically, they are better capitalists. In peace, Southerners are more fruitful; in war, more courageous. More importantly, Southerners invented America. That is, Southerners wrote the Constitution, gave us the Bill of Rights, and gave voice to Manifest Destiny before it had a name. Last, but certainly not least, Southerners have better manners than those loutish Yankees.

Okay, I admit that I have misstated one or two of Johnson's points. He never says that Northerners are tone deaf. I apologize. That was unmannerly of me, a Southerner originally from the great state of Tennessee, where the women are the *most delectable* of all. However, I trust that the reader has caught my drift. But just in case, let me illustrate with a brief anecdote (as true Southerners are wont to do, and do better than anyone else, according to Johnson). A few years back, a friend of mine here in South Carolina acquired for himself one of those mail-order brides from Russia. Let's call her Natasha. Natasha hailed from a fair-sized town called Kirov, and was proud of it. She had spent a good deal of time in Moscow, of which she was equally proud. While visiting my friend (call him Richard) and his new bride, I quickly discovered (much to my astonishment) that nearly everything in Kirov, or Moscow, was better than here in America. Kirovian cuisine was tastier and prepared with healthier ingredients. Even the McDonald's in Moscow, I learned, was better than ours. In the Moscow shops, women's fashions were of a far better quality. In Kirov, the summers were lovelier, and the good folk there, it seems, were politer than Carolinians. And Russian men, in general, were more virile. Thus, duly instructed, over the course of several visits, in the superiority of all things Russian, I have since neglected to partake of Richard's hospitality as often as I should.

What is the moral of this anecdote? Just this: While it is admirable to speak occasionally of your country and kinfolk with pride, doing so boastfully and habitually may leave you friendless.

Much of *The Politically Incorrect Guide to the South* is given over to such defensive boasting about the South, and if it was written to educate our friends in the North and elsewhere, they are not likely to take well to Johnson's suggestion (Chapter 14) that they "thank God for the South." Frankly, I have some difficulty imagining New Yorkers or Iowans or Oregonians sitting down to what they call "dinner" and thanking the good Lord for "these thy gifts and those good Southerners to whom we owe so much." No, I don't think that Johnson or his publisher really imagined that copies of this book would be flying off the shelves in Vermont or Indiana or California. My local Books-a-Million, however, probably has them stacked in pyramids in the front of the store, right next to a similarly stacked pile of Neal Thompson's *Driving with the Devil*. In other words, unless I am sorely mistaken, most readers of this guide will be a certain kind of Southerner, the kind who isn't content in his southern pride, but who must habitually feed it with invidious comparisons to those less privileged regions where the benighted invent mean stories about us out of secret envy at our possession of so many of the Lord's blessings.

To be fair, it is quite true that the South has been the nation's most maligned region, and well before Mr. Lincoln's war. Johnson says in his Introduction that his chief aim is to "even the score." To the extent that evening the score means correcting misconceptions and exposing anti-southern myths, his intentions are laudable. Indeed, he does a fair amount of that, and the curious Northerner who manages to acquire a copy of this book will no doubt learn some salutary facts. For example, he will learn that "most of the 500,000 African slaves transported to Southern plantations came in Northern-owned ships." Indeed, he may—if he is a Rhode

Islander—be dismayed to learn that ships bearing the Rhode Island flag were more numerous in the slave trade than ships bearing the flag of any other state (though New York could boast of being the trade's principal port). He will also note (with hand-wringing and lamentation, we hope) that that most progressive of Ivy League universities, Brown, was heavily endowed by a prominent family of slave merchants back when it was still called Rhode Island College. In fact (though Johnson doesn't mention it), at one point in the years before the transportation of slaves was outlawed, as many as thirty members of the governing Brown Corporation had investments in the Negro skin trade. Now such information is not hard to find, but I would venture to guess that not many Northerners are aware of facts of this kind. As Johnson points out, we are still waiting for the North to undertake a collective renunciation of its association with slavery.

Unfortunately, Johnson's attempts to "even the score" sometimes involve him in arguments that are not as flattering for us Southerners as he seems to think. For instance, among the reasons Americans should "thank God for the South," Johnson implies that if it were not for the South, American capitalism would be floundering. Thank God, he urges us, for Sam Walton, "a native Southerner" and the founder of Wal-Mart. Thank God for Sam's "vision for selling products to average Americans at affordable prices." Now call me an elitist, if you will, but while I will gladly rub shoulders with "average Americans" at the Charleston (or any other) County Fair, I will not join them in their frenzy to subsidize the Chinese economy by shopping for jockey shorts at Wal-Mart. When the good citizens of Bentonville, Arkansas build a shrine to Uncle Sam Walton, that is one southern altar before which I will not kneel.

Similarly, the ever-populist Johnson laments the passing of the "old" NASCAR brand of stockcar racing with its "rough and tumble good ol' boys who would sometimes duke it out in the pits ..." and who "posed with Confederate flag[s] in the victory lane." The "new" NASCAR, by contrast, has been embraced by the national sports media, has cleaned up its act, and, as a result, is "boring." Self-respecting good ol' boys are already "grumbling" about this, he suggests, and NASCAR's popularity may be on the wane in the

South. Frankly, I say, good riddance. Old or new, NASCAR drivers were never "heroic," merely foolhardy. If the NASCAR mania fades in the South, perhaps we will once again have some blessed peace and quiet on the sabbath.

Johnson's "born again" southern zeal is also on display in his ardent admiration for the southern martial spirit. I, too, am proud of the brave southern tradition of service, though it is hardly "politically incorrect" to acknowledge (as virtually everyone who takes an interest in military history does) that many of the nation's greatest military leaders were Southerners. But I fail to see what purpose is served by claiming, in grandiose fashion, that World Wars I and II could not "have been won without Southerners" (actually, Johnson says, "Maybe ... but not likely."). And while I do not doubt for a moment that Southerners are still among the most patriotic of Americans, it must be admitted (as Johnson does not) that our patriotism and military ardor is sometimes blind. I am not particularly proud that South Carolina remains to this day a bastion of support for Mr. Bush's war in Iraq (though even that may be dwindling). On the other hand, while it is probably true, as Johnson asserts, that Southerners enlist in the armed services at significantly higher rates than those from other regions, such uncritical crowing overlooks the rather obvious fact that many of those recruits enlist for reasons unrelated to patriotic duty. It is no secret that military recruiters have focused their efforts in recent years upon economically depressed rural areas, many of them in southern communities where factory closures have tripled unemployment rates, especially among lower-middle class and poor whites.

Finally, for those neophytes who know little or nothing about southern history and culture, *The Politically Incorrect Guide to the South* will no doubt be of some value. Its chapters on the slave trade, on the War for Southern Independence, and Reconstruction provide a vigorous corrective to the noxious disinformation dished out on endless PBS documentaries. To provide just one example, few Americans (including most Southerners, in fact) know anything about the nefarious political maneuvering that led to the ratification of the 14th Amendment. Johnson provides a succinct overview of that inglorious moment in American history.

Some may wonder whether I have been a little too hard on Johnson. After all, these "life-style paperbacks" (as they are called in the publishing trade), with their tacky covers and corny captions are not intended to be scholarly treatments of their subjects. One might also argue that I have taken exaggerated umbrage at Johnson's boasting tone. No doubt he intends much of his crowing to be taken as light-hearted raillery. After all, Hank Williams, Jr. is quoted on the cover ("If the South woulda won, we'd a had it made."). I can only respond that the raillery quickly stales (after about 30 pages, to be exact). I'd rather listen to Hank.

EATING CROW

I kneel to de buzzard, An' I bow to the crow;
An eb'ry time I weel about I jump jis so.

My readers hardly need to be told that anti-racism in America has become a secular religion, but lest there be any doubt about the aspirations of its acolytes, the editor of a recent tome entitled *Racism and Anti-Racism in World Perspective*, Benjamin P. Bowser, assures us that a revivified liberalism, free of the racist assumptions of its "classical" origins, must become a "secular religion [that] will create an effective blueprint for creating an anti-racist future where individual and group rights and freedoms can be balanced and maintained through a global and truly well-informed democratic process."

Bowser's dream is already our nightmare. When I hear words like "truly well-informed democratic process" I feel the urge to reach for my .357. Think rehab for racists. Think racial identity caucuses in every workplace. Think propranolol therapy to reduce your non-conscious racial biases. Forget separation of Church and State. The U.S. is now one vast diocese under the authority of the Archbishop of Anti-racism. Yes, the Church of Anti-Racism has its hierophants, its clergy, its numberless drone-armies of proselytizers, its dogmas, its catechism, its rites of anti-racist initiation, its sacraments, its inquisitors and its shrines.

One of those shrines, recently opened with great fanfare, is The Jim Crow Museum of Racist Memorabilia, situated on the Big Rapids, Michigan campus of Ferris State University. To be sure, The Jim Crow Museum is small potatoes compared to high tech, multimillion-dollar cubist shrines like the Museum of Tolerance in Los Angeles (or its franchise in Jerusalem, built upon a former Muslim burial ground). While it uses video technology to enhance its message, it is mostly a traditional, low-tech museum with lots of display cases crowded with relics of the Jim Crow era: images of mammies, picaninnies and sambos; fluffy white teddy bears with t-shirts that read "I love dead niggers"; black children portrayed as "alligator bait"; replicas of lynching trees; life-sized figurines in KKK regalia; signs enforcing segregation statutes. For the visitor who might have managed somehow to escape the last 50 years of anti-racist indoctrination doled out daily by our schools and mass media, there are tastefully displayed plaques that explain how harmful racial stereotypes are, and how they contribute to what anti-racist catechists like to call "internalized racist oppression," which is when you are infected with the racist virus but don't know it yet, or know it but really *don't* know it. So insidious is this virus, it seems, that even racial minorities can become carriers against their will.

The curator, or sacristan-in-chief, of The Jim Crow Museum is one Dr. David Pilgrim, also the Vice President of Diversity and Inclusion at Ferris U. In interviews the aptly named Pilgrim likes to share his conversion experience. That was when he was no more than 13 years old and living in Mobile, Alabama. One fateful day he "bought his first racist object." Curiously, he doesn't remember what it was, but "he hated it and threw it on the ground and smashed it." Nor does he explain why he bought the hateful object in the first place. Later, though, he became a collector of such objects. Pilgrim, I might add, is black, or, at least as black as Archbishop Obama. He notes in a recent NPR interview with reporter Amy Robinson that there are hundreds of collectors of racist objects in America. Many of them are racists themselves. Some collect the objects merely as lucrative financial investments. Others, mostly African-Americans, collect the objects for the purpose of destroying them. Still others, like Pilgrim, collect for the sake of preservation. During a lifetime of avid collecting, he has amassed over 9,000 such objects, which are the core of The Jim Crow Museum collection.

Critics have suggested that collecting objects such as the Greedy Little Nigger Boy money box (a child's toy) and placing them on public display is somehow perpetuating the problem. They assume (naively!) that the racist affliction is part of our "sordid past" (as one of the respondents in the Comments section of the aforementioned NPR story stated), and that the vile objects associated with it should be relegated to the garbage heap. Of course, they have missed the point entirely. They fail to see just how deeply and invisibly infected we all are. Indeed, those who appear to be healthy, and proclaim their health most vociferously, are the most acutely infected. While they may appear to be in remission, the sickness is eating away at them, silently. "We're not a shrine to racism," Pilgrim ingenuously insists, "any more than a hospital is a shrine to disease." But where would hospitals be without disease?

Any anthropologist can tell you that sacred objects are fundamentally ambivalent. They are dangerous; they must be handled with infinite care and used only with the prescribed rituals. Yet they have the power to heal. Pilgrim and his associates insist that their healing mission is purely pedagogical, that their intention is "not to traumatize but to teach." Nonetheless, a little shock therapy can't hurt, can it? In fact, it may hasten the cure. If racism were merely a case of poor reasoning, then pedagogy would suffice. But racism is a mental disease, so sterner measures must be employed.

Thus, at the heart of The Jim Crow Museum is a very special room. Here the unwary visitor must confront the horror of the lynching tree. The tree is a replica, of course. But to stimulate your imagination, a video montage provides helpful footage of blacks being flogged, lynched and incinerated. Amy Robinson reports that visitors leave the "violence room" visibly "shaken." One Rowena Hamel emerges all "choked up." It seems that she lived through the Jim Crow days in Michigan's Upper Peninsula, where everyone was white and such horrible things never occurred: "I can't believe," she says, "that I am 84 years old and didn't realize it…. How could I have not seen this? I must have been blind to it." She was blind, but now she can see!

Dr. Pilgrim is in the paradox business. His anti-racist shrine is perforce a shrine to racism. Removed from their original context and placed in immaculate, climate-controlled chambers behind spotless glass, diffusely lit, all those mammies and picaninnies and gollywogs become, like it or not, sacral objects with an aesthetic aura that works its own spell. For some, like Rowena Hamel, a desirable conversion experience may occur. For others, the objects may produce a secret thrill. After all, if racism is as virally pervasive as the anti-racist propagandists would have us believe, then just about anyone who strolls through The Jim Crow Museum must experience either a soupçon of racial malice or a pang of guilt—or, perhaps, both. And both may be equally pleasurable. On a website dedicated to racially hateful toys (most of which are also on display at The Jim Crow Museum) one anonymous comment declares: "Toys such as the 'Greedy Nigger Boy' (I feel guilty just typing those words) are so clearly vehicles for spreading hate that you have to expand your definition of what a toy is." Forgive my cynicism, but I suspect that whatever fleeting sense of guilt or shame that this anonymous writer felt at merely typing the word "nigger" can hardly be more than what behavioral scientists call an "automatic affective response." Equally clear, though, is that he or she takes furtive pleasure in typing the words "I feel guilty."

Again, my inner cynic tells me that The Jim Crow Museum is designed to produce similarly fleeting affective responses, though the duration many vary according to the credulity of the individual. Yet the museum also offers a transcendent vision of racial harmony to reassure the guilty sinner with a promise of blessedness. After visiting the museum's exhibits, visitors are invited into the Learning Center to "dialog" about their experience. The Learning Center is in fact a kind of New Age sanctuary, featuring a diorama called "Cloud of Witnesses," which depicts the disembodied heads of a multi-racial host of civil rights martyrs floating in the clouds above an alluring vista of lakes and a homey cottage in the distance. In the foreground a group of pilgrims—of various ages and races, all with their backs turned to the viewer—appear to be drawn toward the cozily lit cottage. Red tints in the painting suggest that the hour is either sunrise or sunset; one can't quite be sure. The cottage on the lake suggests an idyllic American homestead, beckoning out of a future where true believers in a society free of racial hatred will gather around the "family" table and, rather than pray, share their experiences—victims and victimizers gathered in a circle of multicultural harmony. The floating heads of the martyrs are all helpfully labeled, so that there can be no mistake about their significance. With one exception, all were the victims of white killers (usually the KKK). The exception is Malcolm X, whose head floats prominently beside Martin Luther King's on the far-right end of the diorama. Can Malcolm X, who spent most of his adult life espousing racial nationalism and spewing venomous racial hatred, be credibly depicted as a martyr to the civil rights cause? He was, of course, gunned down by henchmen associated with of the Nation of Islam. Revisionists like Manning Marable would have it that X was assassinated because he had moved, in the final year of his life, toward a more conciliatory, segregationist position. However, the evidence strongly suggests that X was the victim of a personal vendetta. Moreover, the claim that he was moving toward a segregationist position is itself based upon questionable readings of his final speeches.

But, of course, it is I who am being naïve now, for religious iconography has little to do with establishing historical truth. More importantly, "Cloud of Witnesses," so obviously a parody of sacred Christian art, reminds us why all secular religion is a contradiction in terms. At its heart there is a hollow place, the place where the genuinely sacred resides, or should. It is true that great art can offer transcendence (though the further removed it becomes from the sacred, the more it approaches mere solipsism), but "Cloud of Witnesses" is not great art. On the contrary, it is sentimental drek. So, if The Jim Crow Museum fails to deliver on its promise of transcendence, what purpose does it serve? Whatever Dr. Pilgrim may believe, or, at least, state publicly, the real purpose of his anti-racist shrine is to reassert African-Americans' unique claim to what the Girardians call "victimary experience." In a nation awash in sacrificial claimants, the competition is tough these days. The rest of us must be reminded, endlessly, relentlessly, that however persecuted we may feel, that whatever bona fides we may display—like lepers' sores—before the judgment of a world grown weary of sympathy, our claims are trumpery. It is not for us to enter the Isles of Blessed, not unless we are prepared to "kneel to the buzzard" and "jump jis so."

On Secession Hill

Some years back, in 2007, I traveled to the small town of Abbeville, South Carolina for its 5th annual Olde South Christmas, an event which, to the casual observer, might appear to be merely an instance of savvy small-town marketing—an attempt to capitalize on the trade in nostalgic simulacra of a simpler time. It had been suggested to me that, despite the superficial resemblance to such ventures, I would find a good deal more than nostalgia in the Abbeville festivities. I was skeptical, but my curiosity was aroused by learning that the event's promoters were affiliated with the League of the South, and was largely the creation of Robert Hayes, at that time the State Director of the League's South Carolina chapter. In bringing that inspiration to fruition, Hayes was joined by several of his close associates, including retired University of Georgia professor, Jim Kibler.

When the League first established a chapter in Abbeville, the town had been hosting an annual "Dickens Holiday" weekend in late November, a largely commercial affair promoted by local merchants. Hayes and Kibler were quick to recognize the potential for an annual event of much deeper cultural significance, and yet one that would also generate commercial revenue. Shortly after the first Olde South Christmas was celebrated, with great success, in 2003, the "Dickens Holiday" was discontinued. Over the years, the Olde South Christmas had the support of Abbeville's leading citizens (including the mayor and the local chapter of the DAR) and attracted sizeable crowds from throughout South Carolina and neighboring states during the first weekend in December. While some of what these visitors (and numerous locals) experienced was typical of small-town Christmases all over America—carolers, the lighting of the Christmas tree on the town square—most of the festivities are clearly designed to recreate as authentically as possible a mid-nineteenth-century Christmas and, more generally, to celebrate the customs and folkways of the South. In Abbeville, I discovered, Santa Claus was dead. Father Christmas had reclaimed his ancient place of privilege.

Those who are familiar with South Carolina history will understand Abbeville's symbolic significance. Situated in the foothills of western South Carolina, not far from the Georgia border, this is a town which proudly advertises itself as the birthplace and the "deathplace" of the Confederacy, and (though Charlestonians might politely object) not without some right. For Abbeville County was the first South Carolina county to vote in favor of secession when, on November 22, 1860, its citizens gathered on a piece of high ground—long since known as Secession Hill—not far from the Abbeville town square to elect delegates to the statewide Secession Convention in Columbia. Then, in May of 1865, after Confederate President Jefferson Davis fled Richmond, he took refuge in the Abbeville home of his friend, Armistead Burt. There, he held the last Confederate Cabinet meeting on May 2. (The home today is known as the Burt-Stark Mansion and is listed on the National Register of Historic Places.) But even before those fateful events, Abbeville was already a town of some commercial and cultural significance. Among its most notable citizens during the antebellum period was John Calhoun, who grew up in Abbeville County and began his practice of law in a building adjacent to the Abbeville County courthouse. Clearly then, in choosing to establish a presence in Abbeville, the League of the South could hardly have picked a more symbolically potent locale, or one more in keeping with its ultimate goal of southern secession.

However, Robert Hayes and his associates wisely recognized that the Christmas season is not a time for preaching secession on street corners. As Jim Kibler said to me, "Christmas isn't a good time to be political. We want to celebrate the South, and that eventually redounds to politics. If you are able to celebrate your heritage, you are on your way to cultural independence, which usually leads to political independence." On the other hand, it is impossible to participate in the Olde South Christmas festivities without being aware of their political implications. During my visit, the Battle Flag was in evidence everywhere, and was particularly on display during the Christmas parade, when dozens of Confederate re-enactors marched in formation around the town square, joined by numerous others in period costume, passing out miniature flags to the crowd as they passed. Nor could many of the visitors standing on the courthouse lawn have been unaware of the significance of the prayer intoned by the Rev. Fr. Alister Anderson prior to the lighting of the Christmas tree. Praying on federal or state property isn't much done these days, especially when the prayers in question very pointedly call upon the Almighty to rebuke those who would seek the abolition of Christmas piety in public places, as Fr. Anderson's prayer (in a roundabout fashion) most certainly did.

The Abbeville town square has been meticulously restored in recent decades, and many of the buildings that surround it date back at least a century or more, including the Courthouse and the Abbeville Opera House. I watched ladies in full-length taffeta gowns stroll the sidewalks accompanied by men in Confederate gray; period dancers performed waltz quadrilles and schottisches; period musicians, such as old-time fiddler, Carl Rapp, or Celtic harpist, Deborah Brinson, enthralled the crowds with splendid evocations of early southern ballads; skilled stone carvers, spinners, broom makers, and blacksmiths demonstrated their crafts and generously shared their knowledge; and re-enactors, cavalry and infantry, drilled on the square. One could watch "traditional southron wedding" vows exchanged, or dance the night away at the Olde South Christmas Ball (the crowning social event of the weekend), or worship on Sunday morning at a "traditional southron" service. If, during the course of the weekend, one felt the need (as I frequently did) for a little refreshment of the stronger sort, the proprietors of the Rough House, a fine old tavern on the square, are more than willing to accommodate you as long as you accommodate them. (I couldn't help but notice a placard over the bar bearing a firm request: "If we can hear you cursing, so can other customers, and you will be asked to leave.")

Among the Olde South Christmas events I took in was the annual Abbeville Writers' Festival, featuring an impressive array of southern writers reading from and discussing their works. The roster in 2007 included, among many others, Clyde Wilson (*Defending Dixie; From Union to Empire*); Gray Banks (reading from his recent short story collection, *Hunter's Chapel*); and Jim Kibler (*Poems from Scorched Earth*). But the most notable literary event was surely the young Dow Harris' unforgettable performance—in one of the back rooms at the Rough House—of the poetry of Donald Davidson, one of the famed Nashville Fugitives and Agrarians. I say "performance," for this was not a reading but a recital of several of Davidson's most powerful poems, including "The Long Street," "The Tall Men" (which calls upon Southerners to reclaim their heritage), and one of his best known, "Lee in the Mountains." The latter work, a dramatic monologue, especially lends itself to oral performance, and Harris, a former student of the Savannah College of the Arts and a thespian of striking talent, assumed the persona of the aging Robert E. Lee with an uncanny power:

> And was I then betrayed? Did I betray?
>
> If it were said, as still it might be said—
>
> If it were said, and a word should run like fire,
>
> Like living fire into the roots of grass,
>
> The sunken flag would kindle on wild hills,
>
> The brooding hearts would waken, and the dream
>
> Stir like a crippled phantom under the pines ...

In Abbeville, the "brooding hearts" had indeed awakened, and watched the dream stir, not like a "crippled phantom," but in the flesh and blood of the young and old alike. Hayes, a retired high school science teacher from the Lowcountry, is one of the old, but I was astonished by his unflagging energy and devotion to the southern cause. On behalf of the South Carolina League of the South, he was instrumental in purchasing the building on North Main Street which became the local League headquarters and which also housed the Southern Culture Centre. When Hayes first moved to Abbeville, Secession Hill had become little more than a two-acre vacant lot overrun with weeds and littered with thousands of liquor bottles. The town of Abbeville was on the verge of selling the hillside to developers when Hayes and the Culture Centre stepped in and raised the funds necessary to purchase it. Assisted by the occasional volunteer, Hayes dismantled, plank by plank, an abandoned dwelling that once stood on the property, and began the work of clearing it for a Memorial Park to "honor all the South Carolina men who wore the gray and the women who supported them" (to quote Hayes' words). At the time of my visit, the project had only just begun, but Hayes envisioned a number of Confederate monuments enclosed by a Wall of Honor, where thousands of brick tiles would display the names of the more than 18,000 South Carolina soldiers who gave up their lives for the Confederate cause.

I was lucky enough, toward the end of the Olde South Christmas, to join Hayes and a small group of visitors on a walking tour of Secession Hill. As we tramped about the site struggling to keep up (for he propels himself along on a hand-carved wooden cane like some Confederate dervish), Hayes spoke movingly of his plans. If I still had any doubts about the value of what Hayes and his associates were doing in Abbeville, they were certainly dispelled by listening to his impassioned vision. He explained that the Secession Hill Memorial Park would be much more than simply a monument to the tragic and glorious past; it would also be a place of pilgrimage for those who wished to renew their sense of southern identity, a sacred ground where not only the descendants of the fallen might pay their respects, but where generations of Southerners to come may recover something of the patrimony that has been lost or forbidden to them.

At the foot of Secession Hill there lies buried an unknown Confederate soldier, believed to be from Alabama. What is known about him is sketchy, but it seems that he died suddenly of scarlet fever at the end of the War as he was headed south on a train. His death occurred just outside Abbeville, so his body was—for fear of infection—quickly removed and all his personal property destroyed. As it happened, the Abbeville depot was situated just across the road from Secession Hill, so the soldier's body was hastily interred there and marked with a circle of rough slate stone. To this day, the grave and the circle of stone remain, but Hayes, who has vowed to "have no Yankee slate" on this soldier's grave, plans to place a proper stone there, one which will memorialize not only this single soldier from Alabama, but all the unknown Confederate dead. After Hayes had spoken to us of that soldier's death, we gathered around the gravesite and listened to harpist Deborah Brinson play and sing a heartbreaking ballad in which that nameless Alabama boy laments his own fate ("Almost four years ago I left my home / With my rifle in my hand. / I fought for my land / Against all the Federal might. / But it's a long, long way to Alabama ...."). As Miss Brinson sang (to her own music) those lyrics penned by the Rev. Alan Peeler of Gaffney, South Carolina, I'm certain there was not a dry eye left in the small crowd. We were all reminded of the southern boys that left their homes to fight in Mr. Lincoln's war, the farewell songs of their womenfolk still ringing in their ears, of all the boys and men who never returned, and some who did, maimed and broken. Here in South Carolina, we will never forget, because they are a part of who we are.

***

Almost 15 years have passed since my visit to Abbeville. The town still hosts annual Christmas festivities on the Square, but the "Olde South Christmas" has gone with the wind. The Battle Flag is no longer on display and no Confederate re-enactors march along Main St. This change seems to have occurred in 2015 in the wake of the Emmanuel AME church shootings in Charleston and the subsequent uproar over the Battle Flag, which then still flew next to the Confederate memorial on the State House grounds in Columbia. South Carolina Governor Nikki Hailey initially resisted the removal of the flag, but, savvy and ambitious politician that she is, she soon reversed that position, stating, "These grounds are a place that everybody should feel a part of. What I realize now more than ever is people were driving by and felt hurt and pain. No one should feel pain." One can only shake one's head at the sheer banality of such words. Hailey herself is from a small South Carolina town (Bamberg), but there is little evidence that she has ever been deeply rooted in southern history and tradition. Indeed, her parents were immigrants, so she can hardly begin to understand the pain experienced by those Carolinians who now drive by the State House and gaze at the vacancy where once the Battle Flag flew.

Long gone are the days when the leaders of little South Carolina defied the northern colossus in the name of her independence. Little wonder, then, that the Abbeville Town Council has discouraged the flying of Battle Flags in the Square. Today the Christmas festivities are in the hands of the Chamber of Commerce, and God forbid that any shoppers or tourists should feel even a twinge of pain or discomfort as they circle the Square in search of Christmas goodies or sample the "vintage" wares at shops like the Crate and Quill. There is much to be said for the notion, which I myself have maintained on more than one occasion, that the sense of southern heritage and identity still thrives in the rural South and in its countless villages and hamlets. But beautifully restored little towns like Abbeville are all too often selling their heritage for a "mess of pottage."

Still, Secession Hill remains, and a substantial part of Robert Hayes' vision has been achieved. In late 2018 an 11-foot-high, 20-ton granite monument was placed on the hill just behind the gravesite of the Unknown Confederate Soldier. The new monument bears the names of the 170 signers of the Ordinance of Secession in 1860. With the blessings of Mr. Hayes, the monument was funded and erected by the SC Sons of Confederate Veterans. Along with the engraved names of the signers, the monument features the brief text of the Ordinance. According to the Greenwood *Index-Journal*, among those addressing the crowd of hundreds who attended the monument's dedication was nonagenarian Albert Jackson, whose great-great grandfather was Stephen Jackson, a Chesterfield County delegate and one of the signers of the Ordinance. "Our flag means a lot to us," said Jackson. He added:

> Some people in the past have dishonored it, waving it in people's faces, screaming racism, all this type of thing," he said. "That is not what we're about. That is not what the Sons of Confederate Veterans are about. We are honorable gentlemen, and we're going to wave the flag, but we're going to do it in an honorable way.

A few years earlier, when the monument was still in the planning stages, South Carolina state senator Danny Verdin (R-Laurens) penned a rousing endorsement:

> When this testimony rises out of Palmetto soil, it will tell a wonderful story. Because of the sacrifice of the Confederate soldier, states' rights was embedded in our national conscience—it is still relevant in today's political discussion; it is still the antidote to a reckless central authority.

Such words would make John C. Calhoun, the greatest of the champions of state sovereignty, proud. Calhoun understood better than anyone that the "reckless" power of the central state could be countered only by an equal power, the power of the American people as represented by their states. But our slumbering states can only be reawakened to the powers that rightfully belong to them by the people in their localities, in our towns and cities, in both our rural and urban communities.

In the South, of course, resistance against the central state has a long and tragic pedigree. In no other region has the separatist impulse given rise to a fully-realized political maturity. For many Southerners, the South has remained, since 1865, an occupied nation, only nominally American. To be sure, the number of Southerners who would today openly admit to such sentiments is far fewer than in the past, but, arguably, the South's consciousness of her identity remains more deeply rooted than that of any other region. Indeed, the persistence of a distinctively southern identity is all the more impressive when one considers that Reconstruction never really ended here, but has, if anything, become more aggressively programmatic in recent decades. Yet, when one ventures beyond the suburban wastelands of Atlanta, or Houston, or Charlotte, et al., one finds that old folkways and attitudes still thrive. In the hinterlands, Southerners still speak differently, eat differently, worship differently, and mate differently. In the communities along rural routes and state highways, the bonds of kinship are still more powerful than political, social, or even religious affiliations. Traditional gender roles are still more deeply rooted than one would have believed possible, and the Christian tradition still provides a protective—if somewhat leaky—canopy against the toxic secularism that has fallen like acid rain over much of the American heartland. While I do not wish to idealize the rural South, I would nevertheless suggest that if any truly effective revolt against the secular imperium in Washington D.C. is going to emerge, it will begin there in the countryside and in the small towns where southern identity and Christian faith still persist.

Resistance must begin at home.

*Confederate Memorial, "Defenders of Charleston,"
Magnolia Cemetery, Charleston, SC*

The Last Train: An Epilogue

I. *Whither Dixie?*

It is unquestionably the case that even today, in an era of vanishing monuments, millions of Southerners, young and old, still well up with pride and tears when they hear the strains of "Dixie" played at public gatherings, and especially when they join in singing that immemorial refrain: "Look away, look away, look away, Dixieland." But what is this place we call Dixie? Is it, even in the year 2021, really a *place* at all? Or is it rather a memory and a state of mind, a symbol of something forever lost but still cherished or despised?

The answers to such questions are complex. For better or for worse, the idea of the South has long since been overlaid (in the minds of most) with the most potent symbol of Dixie—the Battle Flag with its 13 stars emblazoned on a St. Andrew's Cross. The South became Dixie in a baptism of blood that will never be washed away. And that baptism left its mark, the stigma of slavery. Of course, all of the original colonies practiced slavery to some extent, and even after the gradual passage of abolition laws in the northern states, many freed slaves remained bound in that condition known as "indentured servitude," often indistinguishable from slavery in everything but its legal status. Yet it is the South that has borne the brunt of condemnation, not simply because it resisted the movement toward complete abolition, but most importantly because it resisted the movement toward the total state that has today reduced us all to another kind of slavery.

Yet military defeat did not tame the defiant spirit of Dixie. During Reconstruction, vast numbers of Southerners engaged in acts of resistance against what they considered an imperial army of occupation. Out of this resistance grew the Lost Cause movement, a movement that kept alive the memory of the South's martial glory, its heroic struggle against overwhelming odds, but also the recognition that Dixie stood for something nobler than the aims of the industrial civilization of the North—for the sovereignty of local communities, for what has been called "social-bond" individualism, and for the sanctity of blood and soil. But even in the midst of that great movement an alien presence was growing. It began, at least symbolically, in Atlanta, the city General Sherman annihilated. From those ashes emerged the dubious phoenix known as the New South.

Year by year, beginning in the 1880s the militant and separatist rhetoric of the first Lost Cause generation was absorbed into a New South rhetoric of conciliatory optimism. Increasingly, the idea that the South had fought for the concrete and regulated liberty embodied in the provisions of the 10th amendment, was replaced by an abstract notion of universal liberty that easily fell into lockstep with Woodrow Wilson's ambition to "make the world safe for democracy." When the U.S. entered World War I, that move was widely embraced in the South, not least by its ministers. One of these, Randolph McKim, exploited the Lost Cause adulation of Robert E. Lee to call upon Southerners to regard the war against Germany as another sacred cause much like the struggle against northern aggression. Rev. McKim insisted that "Germany must be crushed if civilization is to be saved—if the world is to be made safe for Democracy." Mr. Wilson's crusade, he asserted, must become a holy cause for all Americans. Those who opposed entry into the European conflict he attacked as "weak-kneed, chicken-hearted, white-livered …" pacifists. And if the pacifists' opposition to the war "be correct," he asked, "how could Robert E. Lee have been such a saint as he was?"[1] Incredibly, McKim had served under Lee as a young Lieutenant, and had even published a book on the General (*The Soul of Lee*, 1917).

In the end the New South movement was triumphant for several reasons: First, the economic foundations of the southern economy had been all but destroyed. Dire poverty was common across the racial divide, and many responded eagerly to the naïve (or simply duplicitous) promises made by the likes of Henry Grady (among other leaders of the movement) that the South could embrace the economic model of the North without sacrificing what was best in the southern way of life. Second, millions of Southerners, especially but not exclusively those born after the War, were weary of perpetual resistance and were happy to embrace reconciliation with the North as long as Northerners demonstrated a willingness to acknowledge southern heroes like General Lee and Stonewall Jackson, while leaving the South to control its racial destiny without interference. Third, by the 1920s demographic changes had begun to occur which, over time, would bring to the South a *replacement* population—one might call it economic and cultural colonization.

To appreciate how such demographic changes occurred, we must first of all consider the profound impact of the most important technological development of the 19th and early 20th centuries: the railroads. If one studies historical maps illustrating the growth of American railroads prior to 1860, one will see immediately that north of the Mason-Dixon line, from the eastern seaboard to the Midwest, a dense web of rail lines had already been established, not only local trunk lines but main lines connecting all the important northern cities and industrial centers. To the south of the Mason-Dixon line, one is struck by how little progress this transportation revolution had made. Most of the lines, even on the eve of hostilities, were trunk lines, and were used mostly for transporting agricultural goods to various ports for shipping. It is probably no exaggeration to say that the defeat of the

---

1 The quotes from Rev. McKim can be found in Charles Regan Wilson, *Baptized in Blood: The Religion of the Lost Cause Movement*, 2009. p. 172

South was made possible, above all, by the North's striking superiority in transport. Certainly, the wholesale invasion of the South would not have been possible otherwise. But that is just the beginning of the story.

After the War, and especially in the latter decades of the 19th century, the South became a tourist destination for thousands of northern travelers, a development sparked in part by changes in how the South was presented in northern culture—particularly in mass market novels. Arguably the most popular literary mode of the post-bellum period was what historian Nina Silber has identified as the "romance of reunion." In these romantic tales, northern writers especially (but not exclusively) tapped into an apparently pervasive appetite among middle-brow readers for narratives of reunion or reconciliation between North and South. Such reunion narratives owed a good deal of their popularity to the natural desire for a healing of wounds brought about by the catastrophic losses suffered by both sections of the country during the war. Yet as Silber has suggested, drawing upon the work of Alan Tractenberg, the appeal of the reunion romance was also generated by a number of social and economic changes arising out of what Tractenberg called the "incorporation of America": the rapid emergence of industrialism, the exacerbation of class conflicts, the spread of urbanization, the rise of a new business elite and the concomitant decline of the old gentry, as well as the blurring of traditional gender roles. A profound ambivalence about the desirability of such changes meant that many Gilded Age Northerners, ridden by antimodernist anxieties, began to look with nostalgic longing toward what was left of the premodern South. Its more relaxed way of life, still largely rooted in the agrarian rhythms of the past, its confident resistance to changing gender roles, its contempt for the materialist grasping of the North, the refined elegance of its impoverished social elite, the apparent absence of class conflict—all of these qualities, real and imaginary, exerted an irresistible attraction for alienated northern tourists and readers.

It was inevitable, then, that the "premodern" appeal of the South would be exploited by the railroads seeking to capitalize on the desires of urban Northerners to escape periodically from their anxieties; and it was natural that those travelers would be attracted by the cheap rates offered by the railroad companies, not to mention the growing comforts of the passenger trains. And they came in ever-growing numbers, not just to Charleston or the "exotic" New Orleans, but to small towns, too, like Flat Rock, North Carolina, where even to this day southern belles in hoop skirts enact their fantasy charades. Even as the South itself began to modernize, a substantial tourist industry grew up to cash in on these refugees from "off." H. Roger Grant, in his *Railroads and the American* People, notes that southern railroad companies (though often controlled by northern stockholders) frequently collaborated with northern lines to enable a constant stream of southerly travelers. For instance, the so-called "Cumberland Route" with its ultimate destination in Florida, involved extensive cooperation between carriers such as the Queen & Crescent; the East Tennessee, Virginia & Georgia; and the Memphis & Charleston lines.

As the southern economy began slowly to recover, and with the growth of industries in textiles, steel, logging and furniture building—just to name a few of the most prominent—tourists became settlers. At first, this was a mere trickle, but with the advent of the automobile and the building of interstate highways, the trickle gradually swelled to a flood. Much of this transformation of what we call the "Sunbelt" can be traced to the politics of the 1930s, when, in a manner of speaking, the New South married the New Deal. Franklin Delano Roosevelt had, in establishing the Tennessee Valley Authority, sought to address the persistent backwardness of the South—its poverty and, especially, its racial inequalities. FDR identified the South as the nation's most egregious economic problem, and the 1938 federal *Report on Economic Conditions of the South* stated that "The low-income belt of the South is a belt of sickness, misery, and unnecessary death." After World War II, the dramatic remodeling of the South surged ahead, greatly stimulated by what might be termed its "militarization," as the region rapidly become the home of numerous U.S. military bases and industries geared to military production.

But the changes sweeping across the southern economy were not always the result of outside intervention. Enterprising Southerners by the hundreds sought aggressively to cultivate what some would call a "good business climate," which meant above all an economy free of the burden of labor unions and restrictive regulations. It was out of this new climate that today's booming metropolitan meccas emerged. Once sleepy southern towns, places like Charlotte, Jacksonville, Houston, Tampa and others have joined Atlanta to become national economic hubs. Enormous research and development complexes, like the Research Triangle in central North Carolina, have also been products of the Sunbelt phenomenon.

Between 1970 and 2010 the population of the South grew by almost 70% to nearly 85 million. Many of these millions moved into the South from other regions of the country, most seeking economic opportunity, or looking to retire in places like Florida, Texas or South Carolina. These migrants have been joined by Latin Americans from south of the border, some 60 million of them, most of whom live in the border states, but also increasingly in Deep South states far from the border, like Georgia. (It should be noted that, at a conservative estimate, 20% of these immigrants are illegals and cannot be reliably counted as permanent residents.) Needless to say, such a massive influx of newly minted Southerners has resulted in equally massive changes in the culture, and will continue to do so short of drastic economic and political change.

For all of these reasons, that place we call Dixie is becoming what the Wandering Minstrel, Nanki-Poo, in the *Mikado* famously called himself—a "thing of shreds and patches." The Dixie that seemed so substantial to our grandparents and our great-grandparents, is dissolving before our eyes. In our shiny southern cities, swollen with strangers, one would have to search far and wide to find anyone who would understand what the great Johnny Cash meant when he sang,

> Hey, Porter! Hey Porter!
> What time did you say?
> How much longer will it be
> 'Till I can see the light of day?
> When we hit Dixie will you tell that engineer to ring his bell
> And ask everybody that ain't asleep
> to stand right up and yell!

And, yet, when one exits the urban areas of the South and the sprawling suburbs that enclose them, one realizes that Dixie hasn't *quite* expired, that it is for millions of rural Southerners not simply a nostalgic refuge compounded of "ballads, songs and snatches" (to quote the Minstrel again), but a palpable reality.

II. *The Persistence of the South*

> Because I was born in the South, I am a Southerner. If I had been born in the North, the West, or the Central Plains, I would be just a human being.
>
> —Clyde Edgerton

Okay, perhaps Mr. Edgerton exaggerates. Yet, throughout the better part of the 20th century there was something approaching a consensus among historians that the American South possessed a distinctiveness lacking in other regions of the country. To be sure, there were naysayers, some finding the South distinctive only in its poverty, ignorance and laggard economy. Others granted the distinction but located its source almost exclusively in the legacy of slavery and in the continuing efforts of Southerners to perpetuate a racially divided society. Among these, Harry Ashmore, in his *An Epitaph for Dixie* (1958), suggested that the only peculiarity about the South had been its Peculiar Institution, and that when segregation came to an end, so also would southern distinctiveness.

Yet segregation has long since made its troubled exit, while the South remains a peculiar place, though arguably less conspicuously so. Certainly, Southerners have begun to resemble other Americans in a number of ways that I, at least, find troubling. But much of this resemblance is superficial. The South remains a distinctive region for reasons that are complex, elusive and not easily eradicated. Certainly, the legacy of slavery and segregation are factors, as is the inheritance of tragedy and guilt associated with that part of our history. Beyond these, Southerners are also bound together by a shared faith and a fierce sense of independence that resists the formation of a "mass" society, and which co-exists with an acceptance of rank, as long as the forms of mutual respect are preserved.

Most importantly, though, southern distinctiveness is rooted in its folk culture: its modes of speech; its rich cuisines and rites of conviviality; its varied and original musicality; its arts and crafts; its story-telling traditions; its passion for sport; its legends and superstitions; its humor; and its attitudes towards work and leisure. From the South Carolina Sea Islands to the Piney Woods of east Texas, these overlapping folk traditions thrive, and, despite many local variations and anomalies, they bind Southerners together into a unique people, regardless of race or class. Nor is southern folk culture exclusively a product of the rural South. Charles Joyner, in his *Shared Traditions* (1999), insists that for the most part folk culture is portable, that it also thrives (and is sometimes transformed) in urban milieus. Moreover, the folk traditions of the South are virtually always bi-racial, transcending racial hatred and resentments. As more than one historian has noted, African slavery was a relatively late development in the North; when slaves arrived in places like New York or Pennsylvania, they entered long-established communities and had very little role in shaping the local cultures. Indeed, in the North, they were never more than 10% of the slave population of colonial North America. In the South, slaves were among the earliest settlers. Blacks and whites in the South have always been fellow travelers, and have as often as not lived cheek by jowl.

Nowhere is the reality of African influence so forcefully illustrated as in the history of Charleston, where enslaved Africans arrived with their Barbadian masters in the 1670s. Together they cleared the swamps, shared the perils of the Yemassee War, and harvested the first crop of Carolina Gold, creating the rice culture which would make Charleston one of the busiest and wealthiest ports in the New World. The children of the planters were nursed by African slaves, and the bonds of enduring affection they formed were real, if decidedly unequal. Those same children—especially the boys—shared in the games of enslaved children and, as they grew older, shared the blood rituals of the hunt and thrilled to the same fables and "haint" tales.

Indeed, the folk culture that emerged in the Carolina Lowcountry was a unique blend of European and African practices. If the foodstuffs which graced the table of the "big house" were more plentiful than the fare consumed in the slave quarters, the recipes were often much the same, and often African in origin (think yams and hominy grits). If black slaves brought with them indigenous musical styles, they also adopted European instruments like the fiddle (without which no Christmas feast on Lowcountry plantations would have been complete). Similarly, the Lowcountry dialect was a fusion of English, West African and Caribbean speech; the Gullah of the slave population was distinct but not far removed from the common speech of the masters. Most importantly, perhaps, blacks and whites in Carolina shared a common piety, and if the black expression of that shared faith veered toward a more potent "enthusiasm," it is also true that the plaintive hymns of the enslaved subtly shaped and informed the spiritual lives of the masters.

For all these reasons it was not surprising to Charlestonians, at least, that in the aftermath of the Emanuel AME church shootings in June, 2015, the old city—long accustomed to flames and destruction—remained peaceful and united in the face of the horror wrought by a troubled young man named Dylann Roof. In Ferguson (Missouri) and Baltimore that same year the streets erupted in a fury of barely contained violence after the deaths of black men at the hands of police. In Charleston only two minor acts of vandalism against Confederate memorials marred what was otherwise a massive outpouring of sympathy and grief by Charlestonians from all walks of life, regardless of race. The Emanuel AME church (better known locally as "Mother Emanuel") was virtually overnight transformed into a shrine. The crowds flocking to the church to pay their respects were so large that the city sealed off several blocks of Calhoun Street, where the church is situated, for almost a week to accommodate the throngs. In churches all over the city black and white congregations attended vigils and prayer meetings for the victims and their families. Many thousands more joined the "Unity Chain" that stretched across the city's most prominent bridge.

Of course, it might be objected that had the Charleston deaths been the result of police shootings, things might have been different. In fact, only two months earlier, in North Charleston, a black father of four children, Walter Scott, was killed by an officer in what was clearly an act of excessive force. No rioting resulted. Instead, when the ubiquitous Al Sharpton indicated that he might attend the funeral, Scott's family firmly rejected the proposal, saying that they "didn't want another Ferguson type of circus here."

In its coverage of the aftermath of the Charleston shootings, the national media expressed admiration and surprise, but made little attempt to find a cogent explanation for the city's exemplary conduct. Perhaps the real reasons would not be pleasing to a largely secular intelligentsia which thinks of race relations, or, indeed, human relations, almost entirely within a context of rights and reparations, pitting deracinated individuals and groups against one another in an endless struggle for power and recognition. Almost half a century ago, in *The Lazy South* (1967), David Bartleson stigmatized what he termed a degraded "southern ethic" which, in his view, "recognized no social obligation beyond the familial sphere." Southerners, he claimed, clung to a "pervasive particularism" and had "a total inability to conceptualize social unity in terms other than personal relationships." The oft-vaunted southern flair for courtesy and hospitality he dismissed as "devices for minimizing social friction." By contrast, Professor Bartleson upheld the Puritan example of community, for the Puritans, it seems, "thought of themselves as small societies before they established communities." Real communities, he asserted, "are communities of consent and common goals."

Well, perhaps we are today in a better position to see that communities founded upon mere "consent" are rather fragile mental constructs lacking integrity or endurance. Our Savior's parable of the Wise and Foolish Builders comes to mind. The Puritans, of course, were a formidable lot, but their successors leave something to be desired. Is it really necessary to argue that, for example, the "gay community" is a meaningless coinage? In what meaningful sense can 10 million homosexual Americans, having nothing in common but the collective affirmation of the licit nature of their sexuality, be a "community"?

THE LAST TRAIN: AN EPILOGUE

In Charleston, however, and in much of the South, it is still possible for individuals to speak to one another as "persons," as men and women who are not finally defined by race, caste, gender or sexual orientation but by a selfhood rooted in family and local community and, most importantly, by a mutuality made possible only by the awareness that each of us is the unique creation of a loving and forgiving God. Thus, the most important reason for Charleston's unanimity in the aftermath of the Mother Emanuel shootings was the magnificent act of public forgiveness extended by the families of the nine victims. In an astounding act of moral generosity, the families set an example that will not soon be forgotten.

Beyond that was the simple fact that Charlestonians, black and white, as I have noted, share a great deal that transcends race—a common faith and culture that allows us to talk to each other, that nourishes a level of trust and genuine tolerance difficult to find in many regions of the country. This is not to deny that racial divisions and animosities still exist, but it is to assert we deal with these in our own way, one that includes a good deal of humor and forbearance. I can readily concede that a "pervasive particularism" stripped of any mooring in transcendent reality will almost certainly result in suffocating moral self-enclosure. But as that wise Russian Nicolas Berdyaev noted many years ago, moral life must be "centered in the person and not in generalities. Personality is a higher value than the state, the nation, [or] mankind...." It emerges out of the family, which is not simply a biological order but one of love and sacrifice, and finds its apotheosis not in some "bloodless and abstract spiritualism," but in the particularity of a God who is Himself three persons, who extended the ultimate act of forgiveness at a particular place and time, so that the scattered and degraded human flock might find a perfect and lasting unity.

III. *The Fragments of a Wreck*

Finally, it remains to say a word about the power of remembrance. Let us return to the years just after the great defeat. On May 10, 1871 the Rev. John L. Girardeau, at that time pastor of the Zion Presbyterian

Church in Charleston, delivered a Confederate Memorial Day address at Magnolia Cemetery on the western bank of the Cooper River. That gathering was also the occasion of the re-interment of 84 soldiers who served in Kershaw's Brigade, not quite a third of the roughly 300 South Carolinians slain at Gettysburg in 1863. After that fateful battle, the Confederate dead had been hastily buried in the poorly marked graves reserved for "traitors," but were recovered by the diligent efforts of the Ladies Memorial Association of Charleston. Rev. Girardeau's address was remarkable in enunciating many of the themes that would become, over the course of next several decades, the central motifs of the Lost Cause movement's public oratory and literature.[2]

Interestingly, Girardeau does not waste breath blaming those who left the bodies of these dead "to sleep apart." Indeed, the Confederate dead were, he asserts, "a peculiar people," a people set apart, so it was not inappropriate that they should have slept apart "in death, as in life, adhering to a noble and sacred, though a despised and execrated, Cause." But having been returned to their native soil, they would have a fellowship in death that had been denied them, their dying wish fulfilled by the efforts of their "country women, who with gentle hands removed them from alien graves...." He calls upon Carolinians to award these dead the same honor that would have been theirs had they returned as conquering heroes, for they are the heroes of a "defeated but glorious cause," though they themselves never knew defeat, for they died never having "looked at a conqueror's flag flying over the citadels of a sovereign state." Fitting also it is that they should lie among those who defended "yonder battered and ragged fortress which, though often assaulted was never carried by storm"—a clear allusion to the ruins of Ft. Sumter, not quite visible a few miles away near the mouth of Charleston harbor.

His preliminary remarks concluded, Girardeau delivered a lengthy polemic that might seem inappropriate for a funeral oration. One would certainly expect some words about the nature of the cause for which the Gettysburg dead sacrificed their lives, but he went well beyond

---

[2] Rev. Girardeau's lengthy address may be read in full at https://www.sciway3.net/sc-csa/cemetery/reburyaddress.html

that—mounting what was in fact a frontal assault against those forces of radicalism that, in his view, were the cause of the War, and which, in 1871, continued to threaten the identity of the southern people and their way of life.

"Deep as is the grief," he intones, "we are not here just as mourners of the dead. There are living issues which emerge from these graves [which]... demand our earnest attention." Given the broader context in which this Confederate Memorial Day service took place, we can be sure that Girardeau's audience was prepared and expectant; they had not come simply to hear the dead eulogized. He asks his audience a question which must have been a pressing one for those Southerners who survived the conflict, who found much of their world and all of their aspirations reduced to rubble. It is the question out of which the Lost Cause movement originated: "Was this sacrifice a useless one? Was this precious blood spilt in vain?" If the Confederate dead were truly rebels against "lawful authority," then the "principles upon which they acted ought to be abandoned."

But Girardeau clearly did not believe that the authority against which they struggled was "lawful"; nor did he believe that those principles which drove them into the teeth of the Federal guns at Gettysburg should be abandoned. For the forces against which they struggled were awakened by a spirit of radicalism that began in Europe and spread like an alien infection to the United States. By "radicalism" he refers to an ideology (and its agents) of anarchic revolt against the natural and harmonious order of family, state, and church. But more generally he seems to mean any egalitarian force that would dissolve natural hierarchies: The "ruthless, leveling spirit ..." of radicalism wages war against "Hearth-stones, graves, altars, [and] temples—all ... borne down under its tempestuous irruption. Nothing is safe from it. There is no sanctuary it will not invade, no just, holy, time-honored sanction it will not violate." While he never refers explicitly to the Abolitionists, it is evident that they embodied the spirit of anarchic radicalism which had swept away the constitutional principles of the Founders. It was this spirit, he argues, that overrode "every moral and constitutional obstacle which opposed its progress...." It was this same spirit of radicalism that made government the instrument of a "faction" and then proceeded to pervert the original intent of the Constitution, particularly the guarantee of autonomy to the States. Thus, the Confederate dead were not rebels against lawful authority; they were in fact the champions of liberty against the usurpers of lawful authority.

Yet Girardeau's polemic probes deeper still. Echoing John C. Calhoun, he argues that effective government answers to two fundamental human wants: "liberty and protection." Of these, the need for protection, or security, is the more fundamental. When the spirit of liberty becomes "the desolating misrule of anarchy," then the people who suffer under its sway will seek protection in "Despotism." But the habits of unregulated liberty are not so easily suppressed. The likely result is a "mechanical union between the imperial and the popular element"— a "Democratic Absolutism." Girardeau seems to be thinking here of Napoleon III, but he implies that the emergence of the Republican party-state monolith under Lincoln and his successor was also a union of popular and imperial elements. This "iron body attached to feet of clay," he ventures to prophesy, may in the not so distant future bring the whole of the civilized world under its totalitarian sway, a "great Imperial Despotism resting upon the uncertain masses of a fierce democracy." In short, Girardeau adumbrates, in language approaching the apocalyptic, an updated image of the Hobbesian Leviathan, which is also an image of the Anti-Christ. It was against this Leviathan state, which sought to eradicate the *regulated* liberties of free men in the name of a radically egalitarian social agenda, that the Confederacy struggled and lost.

However, Girardeau insists, the Confederate *cause* is not lost. The principle of regulated liberty can never be truly lost, unless the people themselves relinquish it: "It behooves us to cling [to that principle] as drowning men to the fragments of a wreck." He urges his listeners to "preserve an attitude of protest against those Radical influences which threaten to sweep away every vestige of constitutional rights and guarantees ...." Discreetly, he says, "I presume not to speak of special political measures ..." but, in what sounds very much like a modus operandi for the Lost Cause movement, he urges that an attitude of protest must begin with strenuous efforts to "maintain our identity as a people." This identity is in danger of being lost, of being "swallowed up in that of a people which, having despoiled us of the rights of freemen, assumes to do our thinking, our legislating, and our ruling for us." We must also, he insists, "continue to wear the badge of mourning" which distinguishes us from a people "inflated with material prosperity." Moreover, we must transform the "sufferings endured for freedom's sake into a discipline that will save our virtues from decay." Southern identity must be preserved by instituting peculiar customs and organizations which will discharge the office of monuments perpetuating the past; by forming associations of a memorial character like that whose call gathers us here today; by collecting and publishing materials for our own history; and by appointing anniversaries by which ... we can commemorate the deeds of men who died for our fundamental liberties and constitutional rights. We may do it, by scrupulously adhering to the phraseology of the past — by making it the vehicle for transmitting to our posterity ideas which once true are true forever.... We may do it by the education we impart to the young; by making our nurseries, schools and colleges channels for conveying from generation to generation our own type of thought, sentiment and opinion; by stamping on the minds of our children principles hallowed by the blood of patriots.

It should be clear that for Girardeau the Lost Cause was primarily a *continuing* struggle, and as it was for him, so it should be for us—we who face today a far subtler and more insidious antagonist. In the words of Charleston poet Henry Timrod, we must cling to the memory of those who died, but not in vain, in "meadows beaten into bloody clay."

General Robert E. Lee

Acknowledgements

"In All the Ancient Circles," first published in *The Abbeville Review*, Sept. 2014

"Of Monkeys and Mermaids," first published in *Chronicles: A Magazine of American Culture*, Nov. 2011

"The Strange Career of Segregation," presented at the Abbeville Institute Summer School, July 2019, Seabrook Island, SC

"The Faces of Men," first published in *Chronicles: A Magazine of American Culture*, Sept. 2007

"Zora Neale Hurston's White Mare," first published in *Chronicles: A Magazine of American Culture*, March 2012

"The Crossroads Merchants," first published in *Chronicles: A Magazine of American Culture*, Oct. 2016

"GOP Country," first published in *Chronicles: A Magazine of American Culture*, Oct. 2007

"Books Are for Blockheads," first published in *Chronicles: A Magazine of American Culture*, Aug. 2013

"The Flamingo Kid," first published in *Chronicles: A Magazine of American Culture*, Oct. 2005

"Dixie for Dummies," first published in *Chronicles: A Magazine of American Culture*, June 2007

"Eating Crow," first published in *Chronicles: A Magazine of American Culture*, Oct. 2013

"On Secession Hill," first published in *Chronicles: A Magazine of American Culture* as "Christmas in Abbeville," June 2008

"The Last Train: An Epilogue," includes material from "Persons, Places, and Things," first published in *Chronicles: A Magazine of American Culture*, Apr. 2016, and "The Graves of Thermopylae," a talk presented at the Abbeville Institute Summer School on the New South, July 2019

About the Author

Jack Trotter is a professor of English Literature, a freelance editor, a frequent writer for *Chronicles: A Magazine of American Culture* and a contributing scholar at the Abbeville Institute. He is a native of Tennessee but has resided for many years in Charleston, SC.

Available From Shotwell Publishing

If you enjoyed this book, perhaps some of our other titles will pique your interest. The following titles are now available for your reading pleasure… Enjoy!

MARK C. ATKINS
WOMEN IN COMBAT
Feminism Goes to War

JOYCE BENNETT
MARYLAND, MY MARYLAND
The Cultural Cleansing of a Small Southern State

GARRY BOWERS
SLAVERY AND THE CIVIL WAR
What Your History Teacher Didn't Tell You

DIXIE DAYS
Reminiscences Of A Southern Boyhood

JERRY BREWER
DISMANTLING THE REPUBLIC

ANDREW P. CALHOUN, JR.
MY OWN DARLING WIFE
Letters from a Confederate Volunteer

JOHN CHODES
SEGREGATION
Federal Policy or Racism?

WASHINGTON'S KKK
The Union League during Southern Reconstruction

PAUL C. GRAHAM
CONFEDERAPHOBIA
An American Epidemic

WHEN THE YANKEES COME
Former South Carolina Slaves Remember Sherman's Invasion

JOSEPH JAY
SACRED CONVICTION
The South's Stand for Biblical Authority

SUZANNE PARFITT JOHNSON
MAXCY GREGG'S SPORTING JOURNALS 1842 - 1858

JAMES RONALD KENNEDY
DIXIE RISING: *Rules for Rebels*

WHEN REBEL WAS COOL
Growing Up in Dixie, 1950-1965

JAMES R. & WALTER D. KENNEDY
PUNISHED WITH POVERTY
The Suffering South – Prosperity to Poverty and the Continuing Struggle, 2nd ed.

THE SOUTH WAS RIGHT!

YANKEE EMPIRE
Aggressive Abroad and Despotic at Home

PHILIP LEIGH
THE DEVIL'S TOWN
Hot Springs During the Gangster Era

U.S. GRANT'S FAILED PRESIDENCY

LEWIS LIBERMAN
SNOWFLAKE BUDDIES
ABC Leftism for Kids!

JACK MARQUARDT
AROUND THE WORLD IN EIGHTY YEARS
Confessions of a Connecticut Confederate

MICHAEL MARTIN

SOUTHERN GRIT
Sensing the Siege at Petersburg

SAMUEL W. MITCHAM

THE GREATEST LYNCHING IN AMERICAN HISTORY: New York, 1863

CHARLES T. PACE

LINCOLN AS HE REALLY WAS

SOUTHERN INDEPENDENCE. WHY WAR?
The War to Prevent Southern Independence

JAMES RUTLEDGE ROESCH

FROM FOUNDING FATHERS TO FIRE EATERS
The Constitutional Doctrine of States' Rights in the Old South

KIRKPATRICK SALE

EMANCIPATION HELL
The Tragedy Wrought by Lincoln's Emancipation Proclamation

KAREN STOKES

A LEGION OF DEVILS
Sherman in South Carolina

CAROLINA LOVE LETTERS

LESLIE R. TUCKER

OLD TIMES THERE SHOULD NOT BE FORGOTTEN
Cultural Genocide in Dixie

JOHN VINSON

SOUTHERNER, TAKE YOUR STAND!
Reclaim Your Identity. Reclaim your Life.

HOWARD RAY WHITE

HOW SOUTHERN FAMILIES MADE AMERICA
Colonization, Revolution, and Expansion From Virginia Colony to the Republic of Texas 1607 to 1836

UNDERSTANDING CREATION AND EVOLUTION

CLYDE N. WILSON

LIES MY TEACHER TOLD ME
The True History of the War for Southern Independence & Other Essays

THE OLD SOUTH
50 Essential Books
(Southern Reader's Guide 1)

THE WAR BETWEEN THE STATES
60 Essential Books
(Southern Reader's Guide 2)

RECONSTRUCTION AND THE NEW SOUTH, 1865-1913
50 Essential Books
(Southern Reader's Guide 3)

THE YANKEE PROBLEM
An American Dilemma
(The Wilson Files 1)

NULLIFICATION
Reclaiming the Consent of the Governed
(The Wilson Files II)

ANNALS OF THE STUPID PARTY
Republicans Before Trump
(The Wilson Files III)

JOE A. WOLVERTON, II

"WHAT DEGREE OF MADNESS?"
Madison's Method to Make American STATES Again

WALTER KIRK WOOD

BEYOND SLAVERY
The Northern Romantic Nationalist Origins of America's Civil War

GREEN ALTAR BOOKS
(Literary Imprint)

CATHARINE SAVAGE BROSMAN
AN AESTHETIC EDUCATION
and Other Stories

CHAINED TREE, CHAINED OWLS: Poems

RANDALL IVEY
A NEW ENGLAND ROMANCE
and Other SOUTHERN Stories

JAMES EVERETT KIBLER
TILLER

THOMAS MOORE
A FATAL MERCY
The Man Who Lost The Civil War

KAREN STOKES
BELLES
A Carolina Love Story

CAROLINA TWILIGHT

HONOR IN THE DUST

THE IMMORTALS

THE SOLDIER'S GHOST
A Tale of Charleston

WILLIAM A. THOMAS, JR.
RUNAWAY HALEY
An Imagined Family Saga

GOLD-BUG
(Mystery & Suspense Imprint)

MICHAEL ANDREW GRISSOM
BILLIE JO

BRANDI PERRY
SPLINTERED
A New Orleans Tale

MARTIN L. WILSON
TO JEKYLL AND HIDE

Free Book Offer

Sign-up for new release notifications and receive a **FREE** downloadable edition of *Lies My Teacher Told Me: The True History of the War for Southern Independence* by Dr. Clyde N. Wilson and *Confederaphobia: An American Epidemic* by Paul C. Graham by visiting FreeLiesBook.com. You can always unsubscribe and keep the book, so you've got nothing to lose!

Rebs
Alfred R. Waud, Artist

www.ingramcontent.com/pod-product-compliance
Lightning Source LLC
Chambersburg PA
CBHW062110080426
42734CB00012B/2821